AN INTRODUCTION TO
THE SONNETS OF
SHAKESPEARE

AN INTRODUCTION TO
THE SONNETS

OF

SHAKESPEARE

FOR THE USE OF HISTORIANS
AND OTHERS

BY

JOHN DOVER WILSON

CAMBRIDGE UNIVERSITY PRESS

NEW YORK

1964

PUBLISHED BY

THE SYNDICS OF THE CAMBRIDGE UNIVERSITY PRESS

Bentley House, 200 Euston Road, London, N.W. 1
American Branch: 32 East 57th Street, New York 22, N.Y.
West African Office: P.O. Box. 33, Ibadan, Nigeria

©

CAMBRIDGE UNIVERSITY PRESS
1963

Printed in the United States of America

40590

CONTENTS

1

THE CAVE AND THE SUN

Sir Walter Raleigh, who wrote the most human
short life of William Shakespeare that we possess,
began his section on the *Sonnets* as follows: 'There
are many footprints around the cave of this mystery,
none of them pointing in the outward direction.
No one has ever attempted a solution of the problem without leaving a book behind him; and the
shrine of Shakespeare is thickly hung with these
votive offerings, all withered and dusty.'[1] Raleigh's
cave of mystery calls another to mind, Plato's cave
of illusion in which the human race sit chained
with their backs to the sun without, and are con-
demned to accept the passing shadows on the wall
before them for the truth—the real truth being
only revealed to the few who are able to break

[1] Walter Raleigh, *Shakespeare* (1907), p. 86.

their bonds and turn to face the light of day.[2] Absorbed in our own attempts to solve the biographical puzzles that the individual sonnets offer us, we remain blind to the sun that casts these shadows but gives meaning to the whole. Begin by seeing that meaning and recognizing the whole as the greatest love-poem in the language, and the mystery of the detail becomes so unimportant as to fade away.

That this is the right approach to an understanding apparently so obvious and so natural, has in point of fact only quite recently been realised; and realised independently and almost simultaneously by two critics, both driven by a wide study of the love-poetry of the Renaissance to admit the uniqueness of Shakespeare's. 'There is no parallel', writes J. W. Lever in a sensitive and learned book on *The Elizabethan Love-Sonnet*, 'in the whole corpus of Renaissance poetry for Shakespeare's sustained exploration of the theme of friendship through more than 120 sonnets'.[3] More significant still is what he calls the Poet's 'extreme capacity for self-effacement' and emphasises as not just an echo of the conventional sonnet lover's avowed humility. As he writes:

Sidney had always his Protestant conscience and the dignity of his rank for ultimate solace; Spenser, regarding courtship as a preliminary to the sacrament of marriage and the subordination of wife to husband, had stooped to conquer. Even Petrarch had sacrificed himself on the altar of love with a certain hauteur— *E voglio anzi un sepolcro bello e bianco*. But the self-

2 *The Republic,* Book VII, §§514-18.

3 J. W. Lever, *The Elizabethan Love-Sonnet* (1956), p. 165.

effacement of Shakespeare as poet of the sonnets is total and unreserved. He has no place in nature or society save that accorded him by the Friend. He is in the autumn of his years, 'lame, poor, and despised', 'in disgrace with fortune and men's eyes' . . . He envies this man's art and that man's scope. Far from planning, like Petrarch, a memorial of white marble to commemorate his love, he pleads to be left forgotten and unmourned, lest the world should mock the man who once befriended him:

> No longer mourn for me when I am dead
> Than you shall hear the surly sullen bell
> Give warning to the world that I am fled
> From this vile world, with vilest worms to dwell:
> Nay, if you read this line, remember not
> The hand that writ it . . .   (71)[4]

C. S. Lewis, the other critic I must quote, proclaims the *Sonnets* not only as unique in the period of the Renaissance but as the supreme love-poetry of the world.

He begins by disposing of the 'cave of mystery' in these terms:

The difficulty which faces us if we try to read the sequence like a novel is that the precise mode of love which the poet declares for the man remains obscure. His language is too lover-like for that of ordinary male friendship, and though the claims of friendship are sometimes put very high in, say, the *Arcadia,* I have found no real parallel to such language between friends in sixteenth-century literature. Yet, on the other hand, this does not seem to be the poetry of full-blown pederasty. Shakespeare, and indeed Shakespeare's age, did

4 *Ibid.,* pp. 185-6.

nothing by halves. If he had intended in these sonnets to be the poet of pederasty, I think he would have left us in no doubt; the lovely παιδικά, attended by a whole train of mythological perversities, would have blazed across the page. The incessant demand that the man should marry and found a family would seem to be inconsistent (or so I suppose—it is a question for psychologists) with a real homosexual passion. It is not even very obviously consistent with sexual friendship. It is indeed hard to think of any real situation in which it would be natural. What man in the whole world, except a father or a potential father-in-law, cares whether any other man gets married? Thus the emotion expressed in the *Sonnets* refuses to fit into our pigeon-holes.

Such is the effect of individual sonnets. But when we read the whole sequence through at a sitting (as we ought surely to do) we have a different experience. From its total plot, however ambiguous, however particular, there emerges something not indeed common or general, like the love expressed in many individual sonnets, but yet, in a higher way, universal. The main contrast in the *Sonnets* is between the two loves, that 'of comfort' and that 'of despair'. The love 'of despair' demands all; the love 'of comfort' asks, and perhaps receives, nothing. Thus the whole sequence becomes an expanded version of Blake's *The Clod and the Pebble*. And so it comes about that, however the whole thing began—in perversion, in convention, even (who knows?) in fiction—Shakespeare, celebrating the 'Clod' as no man has celebrated it before or since, ends by expressing simply love, the quintessence of all loves whether erotic, parental, filial, amicable or feudal. Thus from extreme particularity there is a road to the highest universality. The love is, in the end, so simply and entirely love that our *cadres* are thrown away and

4

we cease to ask what kind. However it may have been with Shakespeare in his daily life, the greatest of the sonnets are written from a region in which love abandons all claims and flowers into charity; after that it makes little odds what the root was like. They open a new world of love-poetry: as new as Dante's and Petrarch's had been in their day. These had of course expressed humility, but it had been the humility of Eros, hungry to receive; kneeling, but kneeling to ask. They and their great successor Patmore sing a dutiful and submissive, but hardly a giving, love. They could have written, almost too easily, 'Being your slave, what should I do but tend?'; they could hardly have written, 'I may not evermore acknowledge thee', or 'No longer mourn', or 'Although thou steal thee all my poverty'. The self-abnegation, the 'naughting', in the *Sonnets* never rings false. This patience, this anxiety (more like a parent's than a lover's) to find excuse for the beloved, this clear-sighted and wholly unembittered resignation, this transference of the whole self into another self without the demand for a return, have hardly a precedent in profane literature. In certain senses of the word 'love', Shakespeare is not so much our best as our only love poet.[5]

There is nothing a mere editor can add to that except to quote what Keats tells us about the poet.

A Poet is the most unpoetical thing in existence; because he has no identity—he is continually informing and filling some other Body—the Sun, the Moon, the Sea and Men and Women who as Creatures of impulse are poetical and have about them an unchangeable at-

[5] C. S. Lewis, *English Literature in the Sixteenth Century* (1954), pp. 503-5.

5

tribute—the poet has none; no identity—he is certainly the most unpoetical of all God's creatures.[6]

As a dramatic poet, Shakespeare has no identity; as a man and a lover he is as selfless and humble as the pebble in Blake's poem 'trodden with the cattle's feet'.

Thus the *Sonnets* are for all time. Yet their poet, being human, was of an age, and in order that the modern reader may not misunderstand the homage offered, I shall have to remind him at times in many of the observations that follow of certain Elizabethan conventions and modes of expression. There is, however, one convention of sonnet-writers which may be set down here in the words of T. G. Tucker, in one of the best editions of the *Sonnets*:

Shakespeare was the poet in 'service' or 'vassalage' to his 'lord', and in the recognised manner of sonneteers, supposed himself bound to write piece after piece to the beloved with a certain continuity of production and with as much variety of 'invention' as possible upon his adopted theme. Any intermission of greater length than usual, any omission to keep up the regular supply of offerings at the altar, would call for self-reproach and apology; it would even supply the poet with matter for the next effort.[7]

And there readers who have like Lewis chosen the better part of enjoying the *Sonnets* as the greatest love-poetry in the world and asking no further questions, may well shut this introduction and pass directly on to Shakespeare himself.

[6] *The Letters of John Keats*, edited by M. Buxton Forman (1936), p. 228. Quoted also by Lever, *op. cit.* p. 186.

[7] *The Sonnets of Shakespeare*, edited by T. G. Tucker (1924), p. xlviii.

2

THE ORIGIN AND QUALITY
OF THE RECEIVED TEXT

But there will be some whom curiosity draws back
to the cave to see what if anything can be made of
the shadows, and who would feel an editor had
failed in his duty did he not hang a votive offering
in the shrine. Such readers must first of all, however, pass three stationers: William Jaggard, who
published two of the sonnets in 1599, Thomas
Thorpe, who stands at the very threshold of the
cave, since but for his enterprise the rest of the sonnets would never have been printed at all; and the
later publisher John Benson, whose spurious edition held the field until the time of Wordsworth.

What was known of the 'Sonnets' before and after 1609
As far as our records go, the first public intimation
that Shakespeare had written sonnets appeared in

a book called *Palladis Tamia: Witt's Treasury*, published in 1598 and compiled by one Francis Meres, evidently one of Shakespeare's admirers who, in a sort of comparative catalogue of English writers of his day and their Latin or Greek parallels, gives a list of Shakespeare's plays so far produced and speaks in these terms about him as a poet:

The sweete wittie soul of *Ovid* lives in mellifluous and honey-tongued Shakespeare witnes his *Venus and Adonis,* his *Lucrece,* his sugred sonnets among his private friends,[1]

and a little later names Shakespeare with other sonnet-writers as one

most passionate among us to bewaile and bemoane the perplexities of Love.[2]

Only a certain number of the sonnets now extant can here be referred to by Meres, inasmuch as some of them were in all probability composed after 1598, while others, as we shall see, are of too intimate a nature for their author to have allowed their inclusion in any selection that Meres can have heard of. But quite a large proportion of these might have been read by anyone, and from among them it would have been easy for Shakespeare or one of his 'private friends' to make a selection for private circulation, as was done with the work of other poets of the time.[3] The sonnets, however,

1 See E. K. Chambers, *William Shakespeare*, ii, 194-5.
2 *Ibid.*
3 See Percy Simpson, *Studies in Elizabethan Drama*, pp. 184-5.

that first appeared in print were numbers 138 and 144, and they belong to just that section of the whole collection which Shakespeare, I believe, would have been most reluctant to see published.

The name of Jaggard (William and Isaac) is famous today as that of the printers and part publishers of the First Folio. It is not generally remembered that the Jaggards had twice before dabbled in Shakespearian copy, after a rather shady fashion—though not one technically dishonest from the stationers' standpoint.[4] Four years, for example, before they published the Folio, though only a year before they began operations on the great work,[5] they had been issuing faked reprints of ten plays as Shakespeare's, only three of which were actually good texts of his.[6] And in 1599 William Jaggard had been responsible for a little octavo book entitled *The Passionate Pilgrim by William Shakespeare*, containing some twenty lyrics, all, according to the title-page, ostensibly Shakespeare's but fifteen of them being by other poets: and even of the five really his, three having been lifted from Act IV of *Love's Labour's Lost* without any indication of the fact. Thus the only new and genuine Shakespearian poems in the volume were the two sonnets just mentioned, viz. 138 and 144; and it is characteristic of Jaggard's duplicity that these are placed first and second in the volume so as to lend an air of Shakespearian novelty to the rest. The text of neither sonnet tallies exactly with its parallel in the re-

4 Provided the 'copy' had been all read by the censor, the Stationers' Company usually accepted it without question.
5 See W. W. Greg, *The Shakespeare First Folio* (1955), pp. 3-4.
6 *Ibid*. pp. 9-12.

9

ceived text, and that of number 144 has so many variants of importance that it seems to be undoubtedly a memorial reproduction. From whom had he got them? Clearly someone intimate with the author.

Two further points of interest to students of the *Sonnets* arise out of these petty fraudulences of Jaggard. First of all while the publication by various pirates of bad Shakespearian quartos since the early nineties shows the existence of a public ever ready to purchase plays performed by his company, Jaggard's proceedings prove that before the end of the century the name of Shakespeare himself had become so well known and generally attractive that a stationer would make it his business to palm off spurious copy as his. And in the second place, what followed from the publication of *The Passionate Pilgrim* gives us what I believe is the only instance on record of Shakespeare, who seemed otherwise completely indifferent to the circulation of unauthorised, corrupt, and spurious editions of his writings, displaying anger with one of the pirates who preyed upon his productions. And even so the instance would probably not have been recorded had not another author, wronged at the same time, issued a public protest.

Jaggard seems to have done so well with the first two editions of *The Passionate Pilgrim* that he thought it worth while to issue a third in 1612. This he now printed under his own name, and in order to give the impression that he had secured more Shakespearian copy meanwhile he revised the title-page and added to the text eight new pieces of verse, this time extracted from Thomas Heywood's *Troia*

Britannica, which he had himself printed in 1609. At this barefaced attempt to pass off more than half a dozen of his poems as another man's work, Heywood protested in his *Apology for Actors* which was printed by Nicholas Okes; at the same time informing the world that Shakespeare, of whom he speaks in terms of noticeable deference, was 'much offended with M. Jaggard that (altogether unknowne to him) presumed to make so bold with his name.' Shakespeare had probably never seen *The Passionate Pilgrim* until Heywood drew his attention to it. But once the book was in his hand he could not help seeing his two sonnets at the beginning. His displeasure therefore may well have been partly due to their publication, and it looks as if Jaggard had the displeasure conveyed directly to him, since he printed a cancel of the title-page from which the name Shakespeare had been removed.[7] It was surely some motive more compelling than a sense of decency or a desire to conciliate Heywood that induced Jaggard to rob his volume of its chief attraction, the attribution to Shakespeare. Further light on these matters is best sought in connection with an inquiry into the origin and character of the publication of the complete text of the *Sonnets* in 1609, a publication which must have displeased Shakespeare far more.

But before actually coming to that, it will be convenient to go forward a generation and take a look at an edition that appeared in 1640 and carries on the story of the piratical treatment of the *Sonnets* begun by Jaggard. Why was it that its editor, while

[7] See Chambers, *William Shakespeare*, i, 547-48, ii, 218-19; Greg, *The Shakespeare First Folio*, pp. 9-10.

helping himself freely to Thorpe's collection, should have spared no pains to conceal both all knowledge of it and any connection with it, so that he succeeded in so totally eclipsing its memory that it was not until Malone published his edition of the 1609 text in 1780 that Thorpe's production took its rightful place in the Shakespeare canon?

The 1640 edition which was published late in 1639 or early in 1640 bears the following title:

> *Poems,* written by Wil. Shakespeare Gent.
> Printed at London by Tho. Cotes, and are to be sold
> by Iohn Benson, dwelling in St Dunstan's
> Church-yard. 1640.[8]

Apart from a few pages of preliminaries, the volume contains all but eight of the *Sonnets*, a couple of songs from Shakespeare's plays, everything that Jaggard had published in his second edition of *The Passionate Pilgrim* of 1612, a reprint of *The Phoenix and the Turtle*, and a heterogeneous collection of poems by other poets including Milton, Ben Jonson, Herrick, and anyone else from whom the editor thought he could pilfer without infringing copyright. That of *Venus and Adonis* and *Lucrece* being still operative, he was not able to include them. And it is commonly assumed, perhaps rightly, that it was fear of infringing Thorpe's copyright that led him to disguise his wholesale borrowing from that collection, although Thorpe's copyright cannot have been very active as he published nothing after 1625. In any case, the work Benson put into the prepara-

8 See H. E. Rollins, *The Sonnets* (Variorum Shakespeare, 1944), II, 18-36, for a full account of this edition.

tion of the volume seems in excess of anything such fears demanded. He laid hands upon most of the sonnets of 1609 but he rearranged them under various headings and in other respects took elaborate pains to cover up his traces. It is sometimes stated that he altered the sex of the Friend. Mr Leishman tells me he made a careful check of the text throughout some years ago but beyond one or two changes of personal pronouns, possibly misprints, he found no evidence of deliberate falsification of this sort.

There is something very odd about the make-up of Benson's volume. It is printed, as it were, like two books, each with a title-page identical in layout and obviously struck off from the same forme, the only difference being that the one standing first bears the date 1640. Yet this first part contains not more than five leaves and consists of preliminaries only, while it is clear from the printer's signatures that it was printed after the rest of the volume, which runs to ninety-two leaves and contains the material detailed above. It seems pretty clear therefore that the material in the first or preliminary part must have come to the publisher's hands after the main book was already in print. Nor is it difficult to see that this first material was a long commendatory poem of sixty-eight lines by Leonard Digges, a poem which was itself merely a longer version of the poem twenty-two lines in length which he contributed to the First Folio; both versions, indeed, refer to the quarrel between Brutus and Cassius in *Julius Caesar* as a 'half-sword parley'. And, this being so, it seems probable that the longer version had been originally intended for the First Folio but was found excessive when it came to press. Anyhow, as it deals exclusively with the plays and never mentions Shakespeare's poems at all, it was quite inappropriate to the 1640 volume. Yet Benson the publisher did his best to make it *seem* appropriate by giving it the following heading:

Upon Master William Shakespeare, the Deceased Authour, and his Poems.

Furthermore, he fills up one of the blank pages with an 'Address to the Reader' which begins thus:

I here presume (under favour) to present to your view, some excellent and sweetely composed Poems, of Master William Shakespeare, Which in themselves appeare of the same purity, the Authour himselfe then living avouched; they had not the fortune by reason of their Infancie in his death, to have the due accommodation of proportionable glory, with the rest of his everliving Workes, yet the lines of themselves will afford you a more authentick approbation than my assurance any way can, to invite your allowance.[9]

This rigmarole suggests to the reader that the following volume was being prepared for publication by Shakespeare himself just before he died and that he had been able to guarantee the purity of the text it contains while he was still living. Considering that what it contains included the whole of Jaggard's spurious collection of 1612, together with a number of other pseudo-Shakespearian poems, this Address is nothing but a piece of fraudulent blurb, and what the writer has to say about Shakespeare's avouching the purity of the verse—the most shame-

[9] Chambers, *William Shakespeare,* I, 557.

less part of it—was indeed that which Master Benson was chiefly anxious to impress upon his public. And the long poem by Digges falling into his hands, we must suppose by chance, he seized it as an opportunity of publishing a collection of Shakespearian verse complementary to the Folio collection of his plays. For he engaged a skilful engraver to make a reproduction of the Droeshout portrait of the First Folio as a frontispiece to face the title-page, printing scraps of Ben Jonson's verse from the same volume to stand beneath the portrait in the lower half of the plate, and introduced other minor features to the same end, so that the whole when rounded off with this additional preliminary matter made a very pretty little book. 'I have become somewhat solicitous', says Benson towards the end of his Address, 'to bring this forth to the perfect view of all men.' He had indeed! And the enterprise was so successful that his edition of the *Sonnets* was accepted as authentic throughout the eighteenth century, perhaps even by Wordsworth himself, while as recently as 1943 Edmund Chambers was sufficiently impressed by Benson's declaration that Shakespeare had vouched for the purity of the *Poems* to observe that 'it is at least possible that Benson knew of some statement by Shakespeare, which has not come down to us'.[10] Nothing, however, that Benson says deserves any credit. His game, apart from selling his book, was to conceal its connection with Thorpe's publication thirty years before, to a consideration of which we must now turn.

10 *Shakespearean Gleanings* (1943), p. 111.

The copy for the 1609 sonnets was entered in the Stationers' Register for Thomas Thorpe on 20 May. According to Rollins eleven copies survive, their title-pages all beginning:

SHAKE-SPEARES
SONNETS
Neuer before Imprinted.
AT LONDON
By *G. Elde* for *T. T.* and are

seven of them concluding

to be solde by *Iohn Wright* dwelling
at Christ Church Gate.
1609

while the other four end simply

to be solde by William Aspley. 1609

—the difference implying that Thorpe or Elde had engaged two booksellers to distribute the copies to the public.[11]

No serious student now questions the authorship of the *Sonnets*. But the authenticity of the text, that is to say how far the author was himself responsible for the copy then printed, is a very different matter and one upon which critical opinion has been sharply divided: though I think most scholars would nowadays agree that the edition of 1640 has no prior claim at all, and that if we were speaking of a dramatic text the 1609 publication would be

11 See Lee, facsimile of the *Sonnets*, pp. 31-4.

classed as a Good Quarto, which means that the copy Thorpe handed to the printer, if not Shakespeare's autograph, was a tolerably competent transcript of such an autograph, perhaps at more than one remove, or by more than one transcriber.[12] Apart from this, and bibliographical evidence to which we must return later, the text offers one criterion of authenticity normally absent from books of playhouse origin. Consisting as it does of 154 sonnets, that is to say of a series of separate poems, or stanzas, on the same or related themes, our decision as to its proximity to Shakespeare's manuscript or manuscripts must be influenced by the order in which the sonnets appear. In other words, if upon examination of their contents we come to the conclusion that certain sonnets or groups of sonnets are in what is obviously or probably their wrong order or their wrong place in the whole collection, we are bound to assume that Thorpe or some other person had originally procured them on separate leaves or in separate bundles which he was unable to sort out correctly, unless, indeed, Shakespeare himself had disarranged them deliberately for purposes of concealment. Most readers, however, will not be disposed to deny authority to one feature of Thorpe's arrangement, namely its division into two sections, the first (numbers 1-126) being written to or about a young man, and most of those in the second (numbers 127-154) being written to or about a dark

12 This is suggested by the fact that the frequent error of *their* for *thy*, first noticed by Malone, 'occurs fourteen times in the series of sonnets from 26 to 70 inclusive and only once besides, viz. in 128', and 'this last instance forbids us to explain it by a mere change of compositors'. (H. C. Beeching, *The Sonnets of Shakespeare*; with an introduction and notes (1904), p. lxv.)

woman. It is obvious, also, that numbers 1-17 were written to persuade the young man to marry and beget heirs, while many readers would agree further to regard the twelve-line sonnet 126, which brings Thorpe's first section to an end, as an Envoy intended as its conclusion, the more so as Sidney concludes his *Astrophel and Stella* in the same way.[13] Thus there seem to be at least the elements of arrangement in the printed text of section I, concerned with the young man. The same cannot however be said of the sonnets which follow in section II. No one, in fact, has been able to detect any order in this second section, which Mackail well described as 'a miscellaneous and disorderly appendix'.[14] It looks, indeed, as if Thorpe or someone else simply threw together into this section sonnets he could find no place for in the other. Further, I shall assume what is sometimes questioned, that the woman to whom they are mainly addressed is the same as the woman referred to in section I, as having had an intrigue with the young man, just as I shall assume that the sonnets of section I were all written to the same young man. The problem of sequence then attaches to section I only.

Now, that certain sonnets in this section are not in their right order is, I believe, certain, though it is often doubted. Dowden, for example, made a brave attempt to justify the 1609 order by claiming to discover points of connection between successive sonnets.[15] But Sidney Lee was able to demonstrate

[13] Chambers, *William Shakespeare*, I, suggests the possibility that it was originally written as the conclusion to the group 1-17.

[14] J. W. Mackail, *The Approach to Shakespeare* (1930), p. 116.

[15] *The Sonnets of Shakespeare*, edited by Edward Dowden (1883).

18

without difficulty the 'over-subtlety'[16] of these links; and Dowden himself admitted that they may have been pressed too far. On the other hand, Lee was certainly wrong in his belief that the order Thorpe gives us was entirely his own, arrived at by the light of nature working upon a collection of Shakespearian poems in sonnet-form drawn from different sources. As against this there is the evidence of the general framework just noted, the initial sequence 1-17 upon marriage, and traces of several other sequences which appear at different parts of Thorpe's collection, in particular the group concerning the Rival Poet and, perhaps most obvious of all, the group (97-126) that concludes section 1 as a whole. By way of showing that while Thorpe's framework for section 1 is apparently sound, the sequence of the sonnets within the frame is not always so, I propose to begin by considering sonnets which are suspected of being misplaced by Beeching—whom I regard with E. K. Chambers[17] and Mr Leishman[18] as one of the best and most cautious of modern editors of this text. He writes:

Although we may, speaking generally, defend the order in which the first section of the Sonnets are given in the Quarto, it may very well be the case that some few are misplaced; 36-39, if they are rightly placed, do not explain their position; 75 would come better after 52; 77 and 81 interrupt the series on the Rival Poet; and Professor Herford notes that 'the three *Absence* sonnets 97-99 betray a frank and joyous confidence hard

16 Sir Sidney Lee, *Life of William Shakespeare* (1916), p. 165.

17 *Shakespearean Gleanings,* p. 112.

18 J. B. Leishman, *Themes and Variations in Shakespeare's Sonnets* (1961).

to reconcile with the desolate "farewell" note of the previous group and with the silence which follows'. In the main, however, the order justifies itself to an attentive reader.[19]

One attentive reader at any rate finds himself agreeing with all that Beeching here says; and accordingly feels free, when he comes to consider the autobiographical events which the *Sonnets* touch, to suggest some other misplacements, and at times to indicate groups elsewhere in the collection to which the misplaced sonnets might belong. Let me quote one or two instances by way of showing other attentive readers how the argument works. All students agree that the Quarto contains a number of sonnets referring to a liaison between the Poet's mistress and his Friend. Now sonnets 36-39, Beeching's first illustration, are thrust in among a group of such sonnets (33-35, 40-42) obviously dealing with the Friend's intrigue, while they themselves confess to a 'bewailéd guilt' or certain 'blot' on the Poet's own reputation which might bring shame upon the Friend if their intimacy were too well known to the world, and so can only refer to quite a different set of circumstances. On the other hand, sonnets 57, 58 and 61 are clearly—it seems to me—again connected with the intrigue sonnets, and I would draw special attention here to the poignant irony of 61 with its revealing last line. Nor, I fancy, does this quite exhaust the catalogue of sonnets belonging to this group.

Leaving Beeching's other illustrations, I hope that my development of his first proposal will per-

[19] Beeching, *The Sonnets of Shakespeare*, pp. lxv-lxvi.

suade readers that there is something irregular in the order of the sonnets in Thorpe's text. I would ask them, too, to agree that the person who prepared the copy for the press had a manuscript containing the framework spoken of above, into which he did his best to fit a number of detached sonnets, and that this best was a clumsy or at least an ignorant best. Nor do I feel it without significance that the intrigue sonnets, namely, the sonnets Shakespeare would probably be most careful to keep from publication, were among those which had to be fitted in. At any rate, ignorantly fitted in they certainly were. Witness the fact that the Poet's outburst 'Take all my loves' in number 40, which one would naturally suppose to have been written shortly after the Friend's treachery had been discovered, appears later than sonnets 34 and 35 which refer to the young man's repentance and tears, leading to the Poet's forgiveness. Furthermore, in 35, moved by these tears, the Poet is ready to find all sorts of excuses for what had happened, and even goes so far as to suggest that he had made himself an accomplice by trying to find excuses for it. This subtle, not to say far-fetched, argument is quite beyond the comprehension of the 1609 editor, as it is indeed of most readers today. He therefore imagined it must have some connection with the 'bewailéd guilt' the Poet confesses to in 36 which, we have just seen, must concern another situation altogether. And I find in sonnets 94-96 an even more convincing instance of insertion by Thorpe and perhaps the best illustration of his makeshift methods. These appear at first sight to deal, as do 92 and 93, with the Friend's liaison with the Poet's 'dearly'

21

loved mistress, but are found on examination to be concerned with another love-affair altogether.[20]

We shall, I say, have to note other possibly misplaced sonnets. Yet if the assumption of a basic framework of sonnets Shakespeare allowed, or did not disallow, be correct, the bulk of the 1609 collection would presumably have been found within its confines, perhaps those of a kind of portfolio, the initial sequence on marriage, as now, standing first. It looks too as if the almost continuous sequence concerning the Rival Poet was also part of it.

On the other hand, among the detached sonnets there might of course be some, apart from the liaison sonnets, that were never intended to belong to the main series. A possible instance would be duplicates, since Shakespeare might well write two sonnets on the same theme, or making the same point, and then decide which he wished to send forward; and this is what seems to have happened in the case of 153 and 154, if these are his. Or, again, there might be some of his early sonnets, love poems, in the portfolio, written even before he ever saw his Friend at all.[21]

Finally, the sonnets are personal, not, as some have believed, merely dramatic exercises.[22] And they were certainly not planned or composed to form a single artistic creation as Denys Bray argued

[20] This is developed on pp. 60-1 and 86 below.

[21] I strongly suspect, for instance, that sonnet 26 was the covering letter sent to Southampton with the fair copy of *The Rape of Lucrece*. After all, if Shakespeare was in any way responsible for compiling the hypothetical portfolio he would naturally have included this fine sonnet.

[22] A. C. Bradley disposes of this theory in *Oxford Lectures on Poetry*, p. 331.

a generation ago.[23] In support of his contention he persuaded many scholars, myself included for a time, to accept an ingenious rearrangement of Thorpe's order. They are letters addressed by a poet to a real person about the relations that existed between them, relations that changed from time to time according to changes in circumstances, often unexplained and generally obscure to us though all of course perfectly clear to both writer and recipient. The only unity they possess, then, is 'an autobiographical one, following the up and down of an emotional relationship', as it was put by Edmund Chambers in a notable essay[24] replying to Bray and indicating in Thorpe's text pairs, triplets, or at times even longer groups of contiguous sonnets linked in sense-content and often, too, by stylistic devices such as repetition of significant words or a recurrence of rhyme-sounds; links that Bray's rearrangement often ignored. Samples of such linked sonnets as Chambers cites are 27 and 28, 44 and 45, 57 and 58, 63, 64 and 65, 97, 98 and 99. I shall be making use of some of these later on; for the moment it is sufficient to observe that these Chambers' links still further strengthen our belief in the general correctness of Thorpe's order.

To sum up: Thorpe, I suggest, had at his disposal transcripts of two distinct classes of sonnets: (*a*) what we may call portfolio sonnets, namely the 'sugred sonnets' known to Meres in 1598; and (*b*) what we may call secret or private sonnets, namely those

[23] *The Original Order of Shakespeare's Sonnets* (1925); *Shakespeare's Sonnet-sequence* (1938).

[24] 'The Order of the Sonnets', pp. 111-24 of *Shakespearean Gleanings*.

connected with the Dark Woman, presumably sent to the Friend but which we can feel confident Shakespeare did not release for circulation among his friends, however 'private' these friends might be.

Thomas Thorpe and the origin of his text

All that has been said so far makes it clear that the copy Elde handled in 1609 was not a text that Shakepeare intended. Incidentally, its disorderly state cannot be attributed to a desire on his part to conceal the intrigue business. He might best have attained that end by simply destroying the sonnets alluding to it, whereas, things being as they are, nothing is hidden and curiosity the more stimulated. We may be certain, too, I think, that he had no hand at all in, or responsibility of any kind for, Thorpe's publication. Such at least is the considered opinion of most of the best modern critics and editors: Edward Dowden,[25] for example, and H. C. Beeching,[26] E. K. Chambers,[27] and G. L. Kittredge.[28] Only George Wyndham[29] among nineteenth-century critics of importance sought to defend the 1609 text, and the excellent Beeching completely turned the tables upon him by pointing out that whereas in the 1194 lines of the *Venus and Adonis* of 1593, which Shakespeare himself is generally assumed to have seen through the press, only three slight faults can be found, in the 2155 lines of the

25 Dowden, *op. cit.* p. xxvii.
26 Beeching, *op. cit.* pp. lix-lxii.
27 Chambers, *William Shakespeare*, I. p. 559.
28 Kittredge, *The Poems of Shakespeare* (1938), p. 49.
29 Wyndham, *The Poems of Shakespeare* (1898), p. 109.

Sonnets of 1609 there are not fewer than three dozen.

The absence of the dedicatory epistle commonly found in printed poems at this period seems a suspicious circumstance in the eyes of some. For myself, an early seventeenth-century title-page set out thus baldly, as if it were an item in a bookseller's catalogue or broadsheet,

SHAKE-SPEARES
SONNETS
Neuer before Imprinted

proclaims itself on the face of it a publisher's 'catch', even had the publisher not called himself in the dedication 'the adventurer in setting forth'. A prime 'catch' indeed!—but not necessarily stolen goods. The entry in the Stationers' Register is quite regular:

THOMAS THORPE Entred for his copie vnder thandes of master WILSON and master LOWNES Warden,
a Booke called SHAKESPEARES *sonnettes* vj,

Clearly, honest Masters Wilson and Lownes found nothing suspicious about the copy; nothing, that is to say, which might get the Company into trouble with the authorities, for censorship was strict and the stationers were under very stringent regulations. Further, Shakespeare's name by 1609 was a well-known one. Was he not the leading dramatist for His Majesty's players? Not that that much mattered, for at this period the author normally retained no copyright in his own productions; that belonged to the stationer, and if he had purchased his copy honestly from the author or someone else, no one asked any questions. Yet I cannot help suspecting that this innocent transaction was attended with more serious consequences than the honest stationers expected.

Sidney Lee does his best to blacken Thorpe's character and conjures up as his fellow-pirate one William Hall, a London printer in 1609, whom he casts for the part of 'Mr W. H.' in Thorpe's dedication.[30] But he can adduce no evidence that the two men even knew each other, and Edmund Chambers dismisses the whole theory as a mare's nest.[31] In point of fact there is no evidence either that Thorpe was anything but an honest stationer. He even seems to have had something of a literary gift. He was a friend of Edward Blount, perhaps one of the leading, certainly one of the most interesting, stationers of the day, who published Florio's *Montaigne* and was probably the principal publisher, as distinct from printer, of the First Folio. Apart from this, Blount's title to fame today is his publication of the first edition (1598) of Marlowe's *Hero and Leander*. He had been a friend of Marlowe's and 'regarded himself as in some sense his literary executor',[32] introducing *Hero* with a charming dedicatory epistle to Walsingham, the patron of his unhappily deceased friend, which is not unworthy to be mentioned in the same breath as Heminge and Condell's dedicatory epistle to the First Folio. Two years later appeared Marlowe's

30 Lee, *Life* (1916), pp. 159-63, 672-85.
31 Chambers, *William Shakespeare,* I, 566.
32 Greg, *The Shakespeare First Folio,* p. 18.

First Book of Lucan translated,[33] this time published by Thorpe, who wrote for it an even more interesting dedicatory epistle, *To his kind and true friend, Edward Blunt,* from which it appears that Blount had helped his young friend by passing on to him this piece of Marlowe copy. The epistle begins:

Blount: I purpose to be blunt with you, and, out of my dulness, to encounter you with a Dedication in the memory of that pure elemental wit, Chr. Marlowe, whose ghost or genius is to be seen walk the Churchyard in, at the least, three or four sheets. Methinks you should presently look wild now, and grow humorously frantic upon the taste of it. Well, lest you should, let me tell you, this spirit was sometime a familiar of your own, *Lucan's First Book translated;* which, in regard of your old right in it, I have raised in the circle of your patronage.

The point of all this will be clearer when we remember the 'cellarage scene' in which Hamlet became 'wild' and 'frantic' after an encounter with the 'ghost or genius' of his father, clad, however, in armour, not

Lapt in some foul sheet or a leather pilch

like the traditional ghost.[34] We shall hear more of familiar spirits later on. Enough for the moment to exhibit the sprightliness of Thorpe's pen which he gave play to again in the famous dedication that follows:

33 I.e. Lucan's *Pharsalia,* book I. This was apparently Thorpe's first publication as he had just become a freeman of the Stationers' Company. The account of Thorpe in *McKerrow's Dictionary of Printers and Booksellers,* 1557-1640, is both defective and misleading.

34 See my *What Happens in Hamlet,* pp. 55 ff.

TO. THE. ONLIE. BEGETTER. OF.
THESE. INSVING. SONNETS.
MR. W. H. ALL. HAPPINESSE.
AND. THAT. ENTERNITIE.
PROMISED.
BY.
OVR. EVER-LIVING. POET.
WISHETH.
THE. WELL-WISHING.
ADVENTURER. IN.
SETTING.
FORTH.

T.T.

For the meaning of this we are left guessing. My guess, based upon one by Edmund Chambers,[35] is that Thorpe procured his collection from a person or persons he had discovered possessed them and that he found 'To W.H.' at the head of the portfolio or chief manscript. In any case whether he found it there or invented it himself, it served his purpose well. For 'W. H.', as we shall find in chapter 3, almost certainly stands for William Herbert. If Thorpe knew this all along, why did he not dedicate the volume to the Earl of Pembroke? Would not that have greatly increased the sales? Undoubtedly, yet Thorpe had a compelling reason as a publisher against it. Had he done so, the censor and the Court of Stationers would not have allowed it without the express permission of the earl, by 1609 one of the leading noblemen of the land. And Pembroke, of course, never could have allowed the pub-

---

[35] Cf. Chambers, *Shakespearean Gleanings,* p. 129: 'As for Thomas Thorpe in 1609, I doubt whether he had anything before him but "To W.H." on a manuscript'.

lication of the 'private' sonnets and never did. Yet 'To Mr W.H.', if not Thorpe's device, was un-doubtedly written by someone who very well knew who it was.

In other words, we must ask: From whom did Thorpe buy or borrow his collection? That, sur-prisingly enough, is the easiest question to answer. For it must have been one of three persons: and, since it is incredible that either Shakespeare or the Friend could ever have allowed or even counte-nanced the publication of the sonnets concerning the Dark Woman, we are left with the Dark Woman herself. All or most of the sonnets in section II pre-sumably belonged to her for if she was the woman I take her for she would have enjoyed the hating son-nets as much as the tender-amorous ones, for they were an even greater testimony to her power. While as the lover of both men she should have had, fol-lowing the precedent of Delilah, plenty of opportu-nity of getting hold of the rest, if they were not already at her house. It looks, too, as if she had come to realise some years earlier that these poems of her elder lover might become a source of profit, since the only sonnets to appear in print before 1609 were those Jaggard used to lend an air of gen-uineness to the spurious *Passionate Pilgrim by Wil-liam Shakespeare* in 1599; and they were numbers 138 and 144, both in section II which ex-hypothesi she alone possessed. Thus, either because she was in want of money in 1609 or because she had been got at by the smart young stationer Thorpe who some-how learned of her hoard, a bargain was struck, and he was allowed to transcribe the *Sonnets*, together with *A Lover's Complaint* which was also presum-

29

ably among her papers. That Thorpe engaged two booksellers to unload his treasure trove on to the public suggests that he anticipated a brisk sale. Yet no second edition was called for. The usual explanation given is that by 1609 the poetry-reading public had grown tired of sonnets: the sonnet craze, dating from the appearance in 1591 of Sidney's *Astrophel and Stella,* being supposedly exhausted eighteen years later. It was declining, no doubt, but Drayton's *Idea's Mirror* had been reprinted six times since its appearance in 1590 and was reprinted three times after 1609; and I find it very difficult to believe that Thorpe was not justified in looking for a public eager to buy a volume of hitherto unpublished poems by the very popular author of *Venus and Adonis* and *The Rape of Lucrece,* both still being reprinted at regular intervals, who was also the creator of Falstaff and Hamlet. What happened? By 1609 Shakespeare was not only a popular poet but had powerful friends at court, among them the brilliant Earl of Pembroke, to whom with his brother the Earl of Montgomery the First Folio was dedicated; and who, as just stated, probably had special reasons for disliking this publication. I suggest, in short, that no sooner did it appear in the bookshops and its contents become known than the printer was ordered by authority to discontinue further issues.[36] For different reasons the same thing had happened to the 1591 text of *Astrophel and Stella.*

[36] Cf. F. Mathew, *Image of Shakespeare* (1922), p. 114: 'the neglect of the Sonnets of 1609 can only be explained by concluding that they were quickly suppressed' (cited Rollins, II, 326).

3

THE FRIEND AND THE POET

*The nature of the friendship and the character
of the Friend*

We can now leave Thomas Thorpe for the time
and pass on to consider the two leading characters
in his copy. We know the name of one already, and
the sonnets to the Friend when seen in the sunlight
tell us much for certain about the other, though
assuredly without the help of C. S. Lewis we could
not otherwise have guessed so much; while the sonnets to the Dark Woman leave questions in our
mind about him that will have to be faced at a later
stage. But at the outset the Friend's name and personality are among the shadows of the cave, and if
we would learn about them, all we have are those
scattered hints which the Poet's love has given us.

The 'love' in question is of course the affectionate
admiration—perhaps adoration would at times not

be too strong a term—of a man of mature years for another man much younger than himself, in this case perhaps fifteen to seventeen years younger. Such affection, though not unusual, especially with men of an imaginative or poetical temperament, may seem strange or even repellent to most ordinary people. And as many readers nowadays, when all matters of sex are openly debated, will be ready to assume without question that Shakespeare was writing about homosexuality, something had better be said about that at once. Though a brief reference to it by C. S. Lewis has already been quoted, and I agree with him, I do so on rather more explicit grounds.

Whatever, then, psychologists may postulate about the love that inspires these sonnets, it is certain that Shakespeare was not a conscious paederast, and for two good reasons. First of all in sonnet 20, which is perhaps the most intimate of the series, he expressly dissociates his passionate admiration from sexual desire, and does so with a frankness characteristically Elizabethan, in such terms as to suggest that the sonnet was written partly in order to make this point unmistakably clear. That the love was passionate on both sides can hardly be denied by anyone who had read the reference to 'hungry eyes' in sonnet 56 or the couplet of 110. And the second reason is even more cogent, namely that a major theme of the sonnets is the Poet's infatuation for a woman which holds him in its grip and with which he not infrequently contrasts the humble and selfless adoration he feels for his young friend. The affection is so absolute that he is ready to forgive his adored anything except such actions as in-

jure the adored himself. And there is much to forgive, for it becomes evident as the sonnets go
forward that the young man is amusing himself by
making love to the Poet's mistress; behaviour that,
as the Poet is really deeply in love with the woman,
causes him such distress, at times agony, as to intro-
duce a note of tragedy into the series, compared
with which the supplications for pity and the lam-
entations that are the stock-in-trade of the conventional sonneteers sound very hollow and insincere.

A genuine friendship such as that celebrated by
Shakespeare is nearly always based upon reciprocal
admiration, together with a readiness to make al-
lowances on the part of the elder for the younger.
When Samuel Johnson, as he often did, declared to
James Boswell that he loved him, there was much
to admire on both sides, but the great doctor must
have known that there were aspects of Bos's character he could not admire. The relationship between the poet Gray and his young Swiss friend
Bonstetten seems to have been of much the same
character. And Beeching,[1] who cites it as a striking
parallel to the friendship revealed in the *Sonnets*,
gives extracts from Gray's letters which express
Shakespeare's attitude with truly astonishing similarity. For example, 'It is impossible with me to dis-
semble with you; such as I am I expose my heart to
your view, nor wish to conceal a single thought
from your penetrating eyes.' And when in absence
he writes, 'My life now is but a conversation with
your shadow,' he persuades us that Shakespeare
spoke the simple truth when he wrote the letter we
label Sonnet 43.

[1] Beeching, *The Sonnets of Shakespeare,* pp. xv, xvi.

But the young Friend had his faults, and the fault that gave most trouble to the Poet was wantonness; a fault to which young men are prone, as Boswell certainly was and Bonstetten also, to judge from Gray's warning against the temptations his good looks laid him open to. But a young gentleman at the time of Elizabeth and James was conscious of fewer inhibitions than a Swiss Protestant, or a Scot having to behave more or less respectably in Georgian England (whatever he might do in Edinburgh). And the word 'lascivious' is twice used of the Friend in the *Sonnets,* while the trouble it led Shakespeare into will have to be considered later when we come to deal with the problem of the Dark Woman.

But had the boy not been admirable in other respects, Shakespeare could not have continued to praise him in 126 sonnets. Nor is it likely the Friend would have accepted this iteration of praise had he not enjoyed receiving it.

Being fond on praise, which makes your praises worse

says the Poet at 84. 14, reproaching him for enjoying the flattery of others. That he gave his Poet a portrait of himself is sufficient indication that he was fond. Is it not probable, also, if not certain, that he was proud to claim the friendship of a leading poet and dramatist of the day? The whole tenour of the *Sonnets* goes to prove that, at any rate for most of the period they cover, they celebrate 'the marriage of true [i.e. mutually affectionate] minds'.

Yet there are two features in this particular friendship which differentiate it from the parallels

34

just cited. In the first place both partners to it were Elizabethans. Perhaps the best thing said upon this aspect comes from the most learned of eighteenth-century editors of Shakespeare, Edmund Malone, who in reply to a stupid note by Steevens upon sonnet 20 wrote:

Such addresses to men, however indelicate, were customary in our author's time and neither imported criminality, nor were esteemed indecorous. To regulate our judgement of Shakespeare's poems by the modes of modern times, is surely as unreasonable as to try his plays by the rules of Aristotle.

That leaves nothing more to be said on this topic, certainly not by a modern critic less learned in Elizabethan manners than Malone.

The other feature which distinguishes this pair of friends from any other known to history is the extent of the gap between their personalities. I am not thinking at the moment of differences of rank or of the difference, spoken of in chapter 2, between the pebble and the clod, so much as of the gulf that divides one of the greatest of human imaginations from his young Friend who, whatever intellectual gifts he possessed, must have been intellectually and emotionally quite commonplace in comparison. How much did his adored Bonstetten understand or enter into the mind of the poet Gray? Still less could the Friend have fathomed the far greater spirit that brooded over him. Such spiritual disparities are often fraught with tragic issues. The love which a Shakespeare or a Beethoven lavishes upon the object of his devotion is accepted by the beloved as a matter of course, as a tribute due to the value of his personality, though that value is largely if not wholly the creation of the worshipper's imagination. And tragedy comes when the youth gets tired of adulation, or finds another adorer, or—as happened, I believe, in this case at the end—just grows up while the worshipper grows old.

Turn now for a time from the relations between Poet and Friend to what we can otherwise glean about the personality and status of the latter. First of all he was, of course, very handsome; it is a theme upon which the Poet plays a hundred variations, without however giving us many particulars, so that there is little to get hold of if one is seeking to identify him. From sonnet 20 we learn that his beauty was of a feminine cast and elsewhere that, in keeping with this, he was endowed with a delicate complexion. This is specially insisted upon in 99 which compares his breath also to the scent first of violets and then of roses. That same sonnet has, too, the line

And buds of marjoram had stol'n thy hair.

This is generally understood as a reference to colour, and Beeching with a bunch of half-opened marjoram blooms before him defines the colour as that of the pigment 'brown madder'. But, as l. 14 of the sonnet makes clear, it is scent ('sweet') as well as colour that Shakespeare has in mind throughout, and since marjoram is noted especially as an aromatic herb, used in the making of scents of various kinds, H. C. Hart was surely right in thinking that Shakespeare was speaking of perfume. Yet he may well have been thinking of colour, too. If, for example, the boy was William Herbert, he may have resembled his uncle Sir Philip Sidney whom Aubrey describes as 'extremely beautifull' with hair 'a dark ambor colour'.[2] Finally, 'buds', while an apt description of the close curls shown in all the representations of Herbert we possess, seems ill-suited to the long ringlets of Southampton. Beyond these hints there is little else to help us in the way of personal description.

More can, I think, be gathered about the youth's rank or social status. That he belonged to a much higher class than the Poet's can hardly be reasonably denied, though many critics have denied it. The importance attached to the young man's perpetuating his stock by begetting an heir is almost enough by itself to indicate high rank. And when Shakespeare writes

Be as thy presence is gracious and kind

he is assuredly speaking of a nobleman. We do not normally describe the bearing of a commoner as 'gracious' or refer to his company as his 'presence', a word particularly associated with persons who hold court and are besieged by suitors.

Sonnets 36 and 37 again cannot be rightly understood unless we assume a considerable difference in rank between the two persons concerned. In 36 the Poet confesses to some fault, possibly a piece of gaucherie,[3] which he feels will make it awkward

[2] Aubrey, *Brief Lives*, edited by O. Lawson Dick (1949), p. 278.
[3] Cf. 111. 3-4: 'That did not better for my life provide/Than public means which public manners breeds'—a confession, as I understand it, that a player does not know how to behave in society.

37

for the young man to admit acquaintance with him publicly. He therefore humbly suggests that they shall part company for a while, and pretend not to know each other if they chance to meet:

> I may not ever more [any longer] acknowledge thee,
> Lest my bewailéd guilt should do thee shame;
> Nor thou with public kindness honour me,
> Unless thou take that honour from thy name.

And in the next sonnet he takes comfort in the thought that, even if separated from his Friend, the love they bear each other, or at least he bears him, enables him to imagine himself sharing in the Friend's 'glory':

> For whether beauty, birth, or wealth, or wit,
> Or any of these all, or all, or more,
> Entitled in thy parts do crownéd sit,
> I make my love engrafted to this store,
> So then I am not lame, poor, nor despis'd.

The sense of social inferiority, general throughout the *Sonnets,* is here very evident; and beauty, birth, wealth, and wit[4] make an almost complete catalogue of the advantages of being born a handsome young nobleman.

A number of other terms or references point in the same direction. Sonnet 96, for instance, warning the young man against his besetting sin, exclaims:

> How many gazers mightst thou lead away [i.e. seduce]
> If thou wouldst use the strength of all thy state!

4 I.e. a trained intelligence, or (perhaps) culture.

Sonnet 101, again, claims that the Poet's praise will 'much outlive a gilded tomb', which I take to be an allusion to the painted monuments beneath which Elizabethans of distinguished families lay after death. And from 16 and 47 we learn, as already noted, that the young man had had his portrait painted to give away to his friend as persons of fashion were wont, as young Sir Philip Sidney had his painted by Paul Veronese to give away to Hubert Languet. Incidentally, Languet's ecstasies over the portrait were very much in the manner of Shakespeare's in sonnet 46.[5] Then there is the Rival Poet who was clearly courting the Friend not as a lover but as a client for his patronage. Who this other poet may have been and how far he seems to have succeeded will be discussed later. Enough at the moment to remark that it was only noblemen or persons of like distinction who were usually courted for patronage in Shakespeare's day.

When pouring forth these passionate addresses to a handsome young nobleman was Shakespeare, then, only fawning upon him in the hopes of patronage himself? Keats, the poet who is recognised as nearest to Shakespeare in spirit and of all poets understood him best, would have rejected such a notion with scorn, if not with laughter. And a charming book on the *Sonnets* by his friend Charles Armitage Brown[6] devotes a whole chapter to the persuasive thesis 'He was never a flatterer'. A. C. Bradley, again, Shakespeare's most penetrating mod-

[5] See S. H. Pears, *Correspondence of Sir Philip Sidney and Hubert Languet,* pp. 21, 42, 77; and Dowden, *op. cit.* p. xxii.

[6] *Shakespeare's Autobiographical Poems* (1838). Though published fifteen years after Keats's death we may assume it owes much to conversation with him.

ern critic, finds it quite impossible to take the language of many of the sonnets as that of interested flattery.[7] Equally positive on the other side was the official biographer of a generation ago who informs us that 'the sole biographical inference which is deducible with full confidence from the *Sonnets* is that at one time in his career Shakespeare like the majority of his craft disdained few weapons of flattery in an endeavour to monopolise the bountiful patronage of a young man of rank'.[8] To me it is a sufficient reply to Lee's aspersion to point out that a poet who rebukes, however gently, a young man for loose living (95, 96), for making himself cheap (69), for his love of flattery (84. 14), for self-satisfaction (67.2), for keeping the said poet up for hours waiting for an appointment he fails to observe (57, 58), is going a queer way about to curry his favour. And we are led to ask whether his biographer, for all his learning in the conceits and sources of these poems, had ever troubled to sit down and think out what Shakespeare was trying to say. For what an attentive reader hears is the voice not of a client craving patronage but of an ardently affectionate uncle or guardian who, while loving the young man for his beauty and grace, both in mind and person, keeps an eye open for his faults, while he has no hesitation in offering advice when he feels it serviceable to do so; much as the humanist Languet does in his affectionate letters to the young and beautiful Philip Sidney: as indeed in that age, when the government of nations rested upon the

7 A. C. Bradley, *Oxford Lectures on Poetry* (1909), p. 332. Cf. his reply to Lee, *ibid.* 312-14.

8 Sidney Lee, *The Life of Shakespeare* (1916), p. 23.

shoulders of princes and nobles, all men of learning and art who were admitted to their friendship felt it a public duty so to do.

But the friendship of Languet and Sidney differed in two important respects from that of Shakespeare and his young Friend. The humanist-diplomatist, well known in all the courts of Europe, was not likely to labour under any great sense of inferiority in company with a young English knight, even though he were the nephew of the Earl of Leicester. Shakespeare, on the other hand, was a common player, by statute classed with rogues and vagabonds, and it is impossible for us to imagine the social gulf that separated him from anyone of noble rank. A nobleman might honour a famous player with his acquaintance, or even his friendship. Burbadge was so honoured.[9] But neither party would or could ever forget that the one was conferring an honour upon the other; the difference of rank was so absolute that nothing could bridge it. One cannot read the *Sonnets* attentively without realising that the friendship between player and nobleman was nevertheless very real, came indeed to be very intimate. Yet Shakespeare is always aware of the social gulf and not infrequently bewails it, reminds himself of it or is even reminded of it by the Friend. One striking example has already been quoted from sonnets 36 and 37. Still more explicit are the following lines from 87:

> My bonds in thee are all determinate.
> For how do I hold thee but by thy granting?
> And for that riches where is my deserving?

[9] See E. K. Chambers, *The Elizabethan Stage* (1923), ii, 308.

41

But this consciousness, I feel sure, is what lies behind most of the passages in which the Poet dwells upon his condition: for example,

Let those who are in favour with their stars
Of public honour and proud titles boast,
Whilst I, whom fortune of such triumph bars . . . (25)

When in disgrace with Fortune and men's eyes
I all alone beweep my outcast state . . . (29)

. . . made lame by Fortune's dearest spite . . . (37.3)

Some glory in their birth . . .
But these particulars are not my measure . . .
   [i.e. are not granted me by fortune] (91)

Alas, 'tis true I have gone here and there
And made myself a motley to the view . . . (110)

Beeching glosses 'motley to the view' as 'a public jester', and asserts 'there is no reference to the poet's profession' and that 'the sonnet gives the confession of a favourite of society'. He may be right, but he rather wilfully holds that Shakespeare never refers to himself as a player. Of the next line in the same sonnet Tucker writes: 'One does not by that profession [i.e. the profession of an actor] "gore his own thoughts", still less does he "make old offences of affection new".' [10] Yet Shakespeare was playwright as well as actor; may not these words tell us what a dramatist might confess to if he drew upon his own experiences or the characters of those about him in creating his plays? Surely,

10 Tucker, *op. cit.* p. xxxv.

42

too, there cannot be any doubt about this, in the very next sonnet,

O, for my sake do you with Fortune chide,
The guilty goddess of my harmful deeds,
That did not better for my life provide
Than public means, which public manners breeds.
Thence comes it that my name receives a brand. (111)

Even Edmund Chambers, who finds attempts to interpret the *Sonnets* as 'largely interpreting the obscure by the obscurer still' takes 'brand' to be an allusion to the old tradition of 'the infamous *histrio* of the early Fathers'.[11] And this suggestion is supported by 112, which begins:

Your love and pity doth th' impression fill
Which vulgar scandal stamp'd upon my brow;

and so carries on the reference to 'brand' in 111.5.

C. S. Lewis[12] finds it 'hard to think of any real situation in which it [the love Shakespeare expresses] would be natural'. Could any situation render it more natural than this humble adoration of an Elizabethan player for a handsome boy of high rank? Yet even humbler assuredly than this situation demanded. One cannot imagine the boisterous Burbadge, for instance, assuming, still less genuinely possessing, that selflessness, self-abnegation, self-effacement, call it what you will,[13] which

11 *Shakespearean Gleanings,* p. 49. See *Cambridge History of English Literature* VI, 'The Puritan Attack upon the Stage', on the practice by puritan writers of quotation from the early fathers when attacking the stage.

12 *English Literature in the Sixteenth Century,* p. 503.

13 Bradley (*op. cit.* p. 334) uses the term 'prostration' but rightly rejects 'humiliation'.

both Lever and Lewis find as the unique quality of Shakespeare's *Sonnets*. It was natural, not to the man, but to the poet, and to that particular kind of poet who has no identity apart from the objects he is continually informing and filling, objects that thus become the creatures of his imagination, one of them being in this case the young Friend. To use an expression too often debased as a cliché, he idealised him.[14]

The disloyalty of the Friend
But out, alack! he was but one hour mine.

It is evident from sonnet 33 in which these words occur that the sun soon became clouded for the Poet, not long indeed after his first meeting with the Friend: for 'one hour mine' and 'one early morn' (9) can hardly point to any length of time. The cause of this change of climate is also evident from the sonnet that follows: the young man has come to know the mistress whom the Poet had loved dearly, and the two had betrayed him.

The *Sonnets* give us two accounts of this incident, neither very explicit because conveyed by hints or oblique references, but telling us enough to reveal the essence of the affair—telling it, however, in two very different moods, one being conveyed by sonnets addressed to the Friend and the other by those belonging to section II concerned

14 Cf. above p. 35 and Rupert Brooke on the Birmingham businessman contemplating whom 'when the mood was on' him, he found 'splendid and immortal and desirable' (*The Collected Poems of Rupert Brooke* (1918), p. liii).

with the Dark Woman who was the mistress. Let us consider the two groups in turn.

The liaison-sonnets, as I call them, do not belong to the 'sugred sonnets' mentioned by Meres in 1598, and intended for circulation among his 'private friends', but, according to my theory of the text, came to Thorpe's hands some other way and in no particular order, so that he had to fit them into his collection at any points that might seem not inappropriate. We may expect therefore to find them at various points in the Quarto. I reckon the group comprises eleven sonnets, viz. 33, 34, 35, 40, 41, 42, 57, 58, 61, 92 and 93, which I now propose to rearrange and comment upon with a view to bringing out if I can the outlines of the story.

It begins, I take it, with numbers 57, 58 and 61 (a yoked pair plus one of Thorpe's stray cattle). The first ('Being your slave') is one of the most beautiful love-poems when read in isolation; but taken with 58 and 61 it gives us a vivid picture, steeped in irony, of the unhappy player-Poet, waiting into the night for a meeting with this young noble who fails to keep his appointment, and does so because, as the player comes to realise, his lordship is engaged in bed with the player's mistress. Giving it up at last the Poet goes off to his own bed, but not to sleep, for there follows the night described in 61, the bitter irony of which reveals the true nature of the personal tragedy of the greatest of tragic poets and does more than any other passage in the *Sonnets* to convince one reader at any rate of his incontestable love for the Friend, who was at that moment robbing him of the mistress dearly loved after another fashion. And when we, who today see the whole world united in proclaiming him the greatest of human poets, read these lines:

> Being your slave, what should I do but tend
> Upon the hours and times of your desire?
> I have no precious time at all to spend,
> Nor services to do, till you require.

What can we do but cry out with the greatest of his tragic heroes, 'The pity of it, O, the pity of it!'

One must suppose that the agonising 57, 58, 61, being letters, were sent to the Friend, and that hearing shortly afterwards, from a servant perhaps, that his suspicions were all too well founded, Shakespeare followed up 57, 58 and 61 almost immediately with the passionate outburst of 40, 41 and 42, in which he no longer attempts to conceal the depth of his feelings, declares himself grievously wronged in being robbed of the woman he loves, yet, still prepared to find every excuse he can for the boy himself, puts the blame on the woman, even in part on himself, and actually stoops to the 'sweet flattery' of 42 and the pitiful couplet of 40:

> Lascivious grace, in whom all ill well shows,
> Kill me with spites; yet we must not be foes.

Believing as one must that the young aristocrat was genuinely fond of his player-poet, who went on sending him all these charming and flattering sonnets, and had begun to realise, perhaps for the first

46

time—for a person like him would have attached very small importance to going to bed with a woman—that the poor fellow was what was called 'in love' and really terribly hurt, he became rather sorry for what had happened, made a clean breast of the whole thing with tears in his eyes. Such, at least to judge from 34, was the next scene in the story which passes on to a calmer, more formal mood in which the Poet finds more excuses for the sinner, this time in the natural order of things, gives his repentant Friend plenary absolution and perhaps is optimistic enough to hope the whole affair was now at an end. But it was not, for as we shall find later, sonnets 92-3 show him still racked with suspicion and tasting the bitterness of Eve's apple; nor was it likely that the Dark Woman, having entangled a handsome young nobleman, would let him go until he tired of her, which last contingency the Poet must have realised was a more likely termination to the liaison than that the bad angel would fire the good one out. Of how it does end we learn nothing in the *Sonnets* though we must infer that the savage or frenzied addresses to the mistress in section II were written after Shakespeare had discovered the liaison or while he was still suspecting that it was going on. Even these however ceased, it appears, after a time. Anyhow in 1599 Jaggard was printing two of the sonnets belonging to section II, and if he procured them from her, it suggests she was beginning to realise that she could make money out of her elder lover's poems, and one wonders whether she would have ventured to do so had she not been pretty sure by then that he had left her for good.

But it is time to scrutinise this Dark Woman more closely. Beyond the fact that she was Shakespeare's mistress, that she had black hair and black eyes and that Shakespeare wrote a playful mocking sonnet to her beauty, nothing is known about her appearance. Nor has anybody ever made an even probable guess of her identity; for Mary Fitton,[15] the one-time favourite with Tyler and other critics, was dismissed with laughter when an unearthed portrait proved her a blonde. The only other guess that looked possible at first sight was Mistress Davenant, wife of a vintner in Oxford and mother of Sir William Davenant the dramatist who, according to Aubrey,[16] used to hint in his cups that he might be Shakespeare's son, since his mother was a very beautiful woman, and Shakespeare used to lodge at the inn on his way between Warwick and London. But Sir William was born in 1606, while it appears that the vintner did not obtain a licence in Oxford before 1605,[17] which is too late for the affair referred to in the *Sonnets*.

All we can know about the Poet's mistress must therefore be gleaned from the *Sonnets* themselves. Number 42 of section I informs us that Shakespeare at one time 'loved her dearly', and among the sonnets of section II we have a charming poem in which he makes love to her as she sits at the virginals playing and perhaps singing to him (128), and another, the octosyllabic sonnet 145, perhaps a song, which seems to mark the conclusion of a lovers' quarrel.

15 See below, p. 83.
16 *Brief Lives,* edited O. Lawson Dick (1949), p. 85.
17 Chambers, *William Shakespeare,* I, 576.

In 127, again, her black beauty is acclaimed as love-
lier than all the fair beauties of the world and that,
be it noted, in terms almost exactly those Berowne
employs in praising his Rosaline in *Love's Labour's
Lost* iv. iii. 254-61. As with Berowne, too, it is her
black eyes that fascinate him (132). Some critics see
her as the original of the gipsy Cleopatra and the
fickle Cressida; and we may surmise from what
Shakespeare writes about her that what the eyes tell
him is what Berowne again hints at as he describes
Rosaline elsewhere:

> A whitely wanton with a velvet brow,
> With two pitch-balls stuck in her face for eyes,
> Ay and, by heaven, one that will do the deed,
> Though Argus were her eunuch and her guard!
>
> (iii. i. 195-8)

Rosaline, Cleopatra and Cressida are all ladies,
but ladies in a play, and it by no means follows that
the mistress in the *Sonnets* was one too. Shakespeare
never speaks of her as a lady and the probability is
that she was a woman of his own class and, one fan-
cies, of much about his age. She was a married
woman, and there is more than a hint that she had
not only broken her 'bed-vow' for Shakespeare's
sake (152.3) but was at times open to the charge
of promiscuity (135.5; 137.6; 142.8). Yet she was
certainly no common courtesan. If sonnet 128 be
not mere flattery, she could play, as we saw, and
probably sing charmingly. And her lover must have
credited her with an appreciation of poetry or he
could never have troubled to compose some two
dozen sonnets for her, or, if about her, surely in-

tended for her eyes. On the other hand, though the shameless playfulness of 151 suggests how their meetings usually ended, we can hardly doubt that, Shakespeare being Shakespeare, what first engaged his attention and could hold it for hours at a time was witty, it may be brilliant, conversation, and more than a little grace of mind. Indeed, though Sir William Davenant probably knew he had small ground for his half-serious claim to have been Shakespeare's son, his description of his mother, the Oxford vintner's wife, as 'a very good witt, and of conversation extremely agreable' [18] shows us what a London citizen's wife might have been.

Such, I suggest, was the dark-eyed woman who held the greatest of all poets in thrall, much as Cleopatra held Antony; and who can tell for how many years it had been going on when the sonnets to the Friend opened? But there came a moment when the woman he loved thus passionately and possessively met the Friend he adored humbly, selflessly, demanding nothing. How they met we do not know. It was probably inevitable, once the Friend reached London; but one cannot believe that Shakespeare deliberately arranged it, knowing both partners as he did. And when it took place catastrophe followed; his love for the woman grew rancid, a Nessus shirt that tortured him yet could not be cast off because she continued to hold him by her physical attraction:

> My love is as a fever, longing still
> For that which longer nurseth the disease;

[18] Aubrey, *op. cit.* p. 85.

> Feeding on that which doth preserve the ill,
> Th' uncertain sickly appetite to please. (147)

And his love for the Friend, once the sun in his heaven, became overcast with suspicion, suspicion that thickened into agonising anxiety and jealousy until in the end, it seemed, total eclipse followed for a time.

And here I pause for a moment to ask myself and fellow-students of the *Sonnets* a question. Does his picture of Othello tell us anything about himself? If Cleopatra be—as many suppose—in some sense a portrait of the Dark Woman, I have often thought that Shakespeare's account of Antony's rapid fluctuations of mood between demanding passion and violent jealousy might be in some sense a piece of self-portraiture. The sonnets to the Dark Woman seem to support this; now tender, now savage, and at times torn between hatred and physical desire. Was his love for the Friend again in some sense, like Othello's very different love for Desdemona, now worshipping her 'not wisely but too well', with a love as selfless and as absolute as the music and motion of the spheres, and yet 'being wrought', so 'perplexed in the extreme' that he was ready to 'chop her into messes'? If he ever became furiously jealous of the Friend, it could hardly appear in the *Sonnets*, though the agony of it does and the possibility of hatred peeps out, I fancy, in the wry 'yet we must not be foes' of the otherwise pitiable couplet of 40.

The pitiful story of the clash between these loves of comfort and despair can be further traced in a series of sonnets to be considered later, after dealing with an altogether different matter which was troubling Shakespeare at the same time.

The Rival Poet and the Farewell Sonnets

How far does Shakespeare's self-effacement and self-abasement help us to solve the Rival Poet puzzle? I reckon the sonnets clearly relating to this matter to be 76, 78, 79, 80 and 82-96, a virtually unbroken series, which suggests that they belong to the authorised framework. In the first four, Shakespeare seems to grieve that he lags behind the fashion in verse-making, that the Friend who had previously taught his 'ignorance aloft to fly' was now adding 'feathers to the learned's wing', that his 'sick Muse doth give another place', and so on. In all this he seems to be voicing the same humility as before, and Lever, quoting 85. 5 ('I think good thoughts, whilst others write good words') and 76. 1 ('Why is my verse so barren of new pride'), interprets the lines as confessions of *artistic* failure.[19] But perhaps the humblest of the series, number 80, which begins:

> O, how I faint when I of you do write,
> Knowing a better spirit doth use your name

is a confession rather of inferiority than of failure to live up to his own standards. And critics have searched in vain among his contemporaries for a poet whom Shakespeare could possibly have feared as a rival. That he felt him more learned than himself (87.7) is not surprising, since he must have been

19 Lever, *op. cit.* pp. 185-6.

52

keenly conscious of that 'small Latin, less Greek' which was all the learning a curtailed grammar school education had furnished him with. But to what Elizabethan poet, they ask, was the compliment to the 'proud full sail of his great verse' (86.1) appropriate except to Marlowe—and he had been stabbed in a Deptford tavern on 30 May 1593 and is therefore out of question unless the majority of students are altogether astray in their dating of the *Sonnets*?[20] Was Shakespeare then so unconscious of the value of his own work as to be prepared to eat humble pie to poets like Chapman, or Daniel, or Constable, or any other of the various candidates suggested for the position of Rival Poet? Or so uncritical of their work as to credit them with verse like Marlowe's?

There is really only one escape from this dilemma. Suppose the whole Rival Poet group was meant to be satirical?

In 1960, shortly before I set my hand to this edition, Mr Gittings, who had made notable additions to our knowledge of Keats's life, published a little book[21] in which he claimed that the Rival Poet sonnets are satirical and proposed a candidate for the rivalry whom I was inclined for long to accept as the most probable yet put forward. He began by noting that the sonnets in question form a progressive sequence which tell 'a remarkably coherent and understandable story without our trying to identify any character in it'. For example: the first two or three sonnets show a half-playful awareness that new fashions in poetic technique are abroad

20 See below, pp. 62-7.
21 Robert Gittings, *Shakespeare's Rival* (1960).

which Shakespeare finds he cannot imitate by changing his style because he cannot do that without changing his subject—the beloved Friend. It is in sonnet 79 that he first begins to speak of a particular rival in whom the Friend is becoming interested; in 80 he calls him a 'better spirit', yet protests that there is room for both his tall ship and Shakespeare's 'saucy bark' in the boundless ocean of the patron's favour. Sonnet 81 reiterates once again that the Friend's surest hopes of immortality lie in the immortality of the Poet's 'gentle verse'. Sonnets 82, 83, 84, 85 develop the theme of the Friend's limitless 'worth', while at the same time slyly criticising the rival's pen by hinting how far it came short of its subject, and more than hinting that if the Friend were not so greedy for praise he would not receive it in such bad verse.

The author of the bad verse that Gittings selects is Gervase Markham, a well-known member of the Essex entourage, a prolific writer of books on horsemanship and country pursuits generally and also of two bombastic epical poems in execrable verse, one dealing with Sir Richard Grenville's fight in the *Revenge*, and the other with the expedition by Essex and his brother to Normandy in 1591.

Gittings works out his thesis persuasively as far as the first eight sonnets are concerned, since it is not difficult to discover lines apparently satirising or ridiculing characteristic passages in Markham. But the evidence altogether breaks down when he comes to sonnet 86. So far Shakespeare had been mildly ridiculing the general characteristics of his rival's style. But in 86 the button is off the foil. He now turns upon the man directly and begins satiris-

ing his personal pretensions and way of life, out-
standing features which one supposes would have
been recognisable not only by the Friend addressed
but by other contemporary readers. Yet Gittings
was unable to relate any of these features to Markham. The rival must be a poet who was known or at
least supposed to have dealings with spirits at night.
The author of *Dr Faustus* might have been made
to fit this, or Thomas Nashe who wrote *The Ter-
rors of the Night*. But not a suspicion of this kind
of thing seems to hang about Markham. Chapman
had been the rival generally favoured by critics
hitherto. Could it be George Chapman after all?
I asked myself. I turned back to see what William
Minto had written on the matter in 1874 when he
first put forward Chapman's name.[22]

His theory had fallen into some discredit because
it was later taken up and exaggerated by Arthur
Acheson[23] and others. But I recollected that the
identification was mainly based on a passage in
Chapman about familiar spirits, and when I looked
at it I found the argument more cogent than I
had remembered. After rejecting Marlowe, who
had previously been conjectured but had died too
early, he pointed out that the first line in the sonnet

> The proud full sail of his great verse

which seemed to point directly to Marlowe, might,
in Chapman's imagination, seem to apply 'with almost too literal exactness to the Alexandrines' of his

[22] Wiliam Minto, *Characteristics of English Poetry from
Chaucer to Shirley* (1874), pp. 290-2.
[23] *Shakespeare and the Rival Poet* (1903).

Homer which, though none of it appeared before 1598, must have been known of and generally talked about in literary circles long before. Minto also noted that Chapman's chief patron was Sir Francis Walsingham whose daughter Sir Philip Sidney had married; and suggested that nothing could have been more natural than for Walsingham to have introduced his favourite to the Countess of Pembroke or her son. But what struck many good critics when Minto first published his book was his quotation from the dedicatory epistle to Chapman's *Shadow of Night* (1594) which claims that the true poet cannot succeed 'but with invocation, fasting, watching; yea, not without having drops of their souls like a heavenly familiar'. It is all very obscure, as Chapman usually is, but it does imply a claim to inspiration from a 'heavenly familiar'—whatever that might mean.

Having got so far, I remembered further that my friend the late J. A. K. Thomson, who gave us that admirable book called *Shakespeare and the Classics*, had devoted many paragraphs therein to the relations between Shakespeare and George Chapman—relations which he confessed can only be inferred from their writings, since Shakespeare never mentions Chapman by name nor Chapman Shakespeare. A good deal of the argument is concerned with Chapman's persuasion that his spirit and the spirit of Homer were connected in a manner more intimate than can be described as inspiration—after the manner, in fact, that a Greek felt himself associated with his genius or *daemon*, or a Roman with his *anima*. The chief evidence for this belief is to be found in a poem by Chapman entitled *The*

56

Tears of Peace—not printed until 1609 and therefore neglected by previous theorists, but describing something like a vision the young Chapman had received before coming to London—a vision in which the spirit of Homer appeared to him and spoke as follows:

'I am', said he 'that spirit Elysian,
That in thy native air, and on the hill
Next Hitchin's left hand, did thy bosom fill
With such a flood of soul, that thou wert fain,
With exclamation of her rapture then,
To vent it to the echoes of the vale;
When, meditating of me, a sweet gale
Brought me upon thee; and thou didst inherit
My true sence, for the time then, in my spirit;
And I, invisibly, went prompting thee
To those fair greens where thou didst English me.[24]

Upon this Thomson comments:

I cannot attach any other meaning to these words than this—that Chapman claims to have been directly inspired in his translation of Homer's poems by Homer himself or (what amounts to the same thing) Homer's *anima* which came to him from Elysium. . . . Have we not got now a very probable explanation of the famous couplet in sonnet 86:

He nor that affable familiar ghost
Which nightly gulls him with intelligence—? [25]

Among other things Chapman affected was to be a Stoic and Thomson aptly quotes the following

[24] Acheson, *op. cit.* pp. 320-1.
[25] J. A. K. Thomson, *Shakespeare and the Classics* (1952), pp. 169-75.

from Burton's *Anatomy of Melancholy* (1, 8, 2, mem. 1, subs. 2):

Cardan . . . out of the doctrine of Stoics, will have some of these genii (for so he calls them) to be desirous of men's company, very affable and familiar with them.

Jerome Cardan,[26] one of the greatest and most widely read 'philosophers' of the age, was undoubtedly known to Shakespeare, so that the correspondence between his words and Burton's is no accident. Both are quoting as from Cardan a demonological cliché of the age. But Shakespeare is of course slyly suggesting, as Thomson observes, that Chapman's visitant, so far from being his good 'angel' or 'heavenly familiar', is a lying spirit, a devil, who 'gulls' his dupe.

In face of all this it looks as if we need have no further doubts about the identity of the Rival Poet. Nevertheless, as so often with Shakespearian biography, there is no documentary evidence to support the circumstantial. If Chapman courted the Friend in verse, no such verses have survived. While as far as we know Shakespeare never mentioned Chapman or Chapman Shakespeare.

Shakespeare might laugh at Chapman, but in this affair the rival laughed last, for the couplet that concludes sonnet 86—

> But when your countenance fill'd up his line,
> Then lack'd I matter; that enfeebled mine—

may be paraphrased: When you showed that you liked his verse I was left with nothing to say, was

---

[26] His popular *Cardanus Comforte* was translated in 1573, and in a 'corrected' text in 1576.

left speechless. We must suppose therefore that the Friend had given some indication that he was willing to extend his patronage to Chapman. This did not, or did not need to, imply a break with Shakespeare. Indeed, sonnets 92 and 93 seem to say that he remained to all appearances 'gracious and kind', which is what one might expect of a great gentleman.

The Farewell Sonnets

Yet the sonnets that follow, the seven 'Farewell' sonnets 87-93, represent the supreme expression of that 'unembittered resignation' which Lewis found the peculiar mark of Shakespeare's love-poetry. In other words they exhibit the Poet in a mood of extreme depression, so that it is clear he had felt the Friend's approval of Chapman as a kind of desertion. And small wonder, for how it showed up the young man's taste! And as I read these sonnets I am sometimes left with a suspicion that there may be a vein of irony running throughout them at the expense of the beloved Friend.

But there was more in it than this. Consider the group in order: sonnet 87, after a touch of spleen, not entirely 'unembittered', in the first two lines, declares that the Friend's love was never more than a free gift on his part which he had every right to take back again, since the Poet had done nothing to deserve it. Speak slightingly, scornfully, of me, says the Poet in sonnet 88, and I will speak even more scornfully of myself, being ready for my love to bear false witness against myself to prove you right. And in 89 he goes still further: if you need an excuse for breaking off our friendship, he declares, I will in-vent faults in myself. Moreover, I will take care you never meet me; and—here he touches the lowest note—

> in my tongue
> Thy sweet beloved name no more shall dwell
> Lest I, too much profane, should do it wrong
> And haply of our old acquaintance tell.

In 90 the mood changes. Those critics who refuse to accept the *Sonnets* as genuine could perhaps argue that all this self-depreciation might be put on: they could scarcely disbelieve the misery of this sonnet, which reveals the Poet in the deepest depression. Hate me! he cries, hate me now when all other sorrows and griefs are descending upon me; let me face the worst at once, and they will then seem petty in comparison. What were those other woes? Beeching asks 'Does this "spite of fortune" refer to the troubles of Shakespeare's company, due to the popularity of the boy actors?' I find a more immediate explanation in what he says in sonnets 92 and 93. But first of all he turned aside in 91 to try another line of appeal. Imagine, he says in effect to this splendid young gentleman, yourself robbed of everything Fortune has assigned to you (your 'measure'[27]), namely, wealth, strength, skill, fine clothes, hawks, hounds and horses—all that gives value to your life—and think how wretched you would be. Your love is worth more to me than any or all of these and you threaten to rob me of it!

So to sonnets 92 and 93, which puzzled me for

---

27 Cf. *As You Like It*, v. 4. 72, 'According to the measure of their states'.

60

some time. All 92 but its couplet follows quite naturally on the wretchedness of 90 and 91. 'But do thy worst to steal thyself away' takes up the desertion motif again, though this time the Poet consoles himself with the thought that whatever the Friend can do he is his friend while life lasts, because life would leave him if he left him. A pretty conceit, but obviously resorted to for the sake of the couplet, the meaning of which is made clear in 95. One of the woes that make him 'wretched' in 90 is a horrible suspicion that in spite of the young man's repentance and precious tears 'that ransom all ill-deeds' as depicted in sonnet 34, the liaison with the Dark Woman was still being carried on without his knowing it. What else can be the meaning of

Thou may'st be false, and yet I know it not

and

So shall I live, supposing thou art true,
Like a deceivéd husband; so love's face
May still seem love to me, though alter'd new,
Thy looks with me, thy heart in other place—

and above all perhaps the couplet

How like Eve's apple doth thy beauty grow,
If thy sweet virtue answer not thy show

which is a development of 41. 13, 'thy beauty tempting her to thee'? Eve's apple is, of course, 'the fruit of the tree in the midst of the garden' with which the Devil tempted Eve. It was at this point of agonising suspicion that, one may imagine, Shakespeare wrote the most famous of all the sonnets, 'Two loves I have of comfort and despair'. It was at this point too, it seems, that he suffered a double loss of his 'beauteous and lovely youth', (i) to the pedant Chapman whose verse was preferred, (ii) to the Dark Woman. And it was at this point I think that for a time he stopped writing sonnets, at any rate to his better angel. And when we come to 97 it seems to refer to some kind of break, the cause and duration of which constitute one of the major problems of the *Sonnets*.

The evidence of the dates
Beeching's date for the main body of the Sonnets

We left the Poet bidding the Friend farewell in the series of sonnets that culminated with the bitter reference to 'Eve's apple' of 93. There follows one of the sections of the 1609 text most difficult to understand, which indeed can be understood only when we discover the person to whom they were addressed. The sonnets that succeed 'Eve's apple', viz. 94, 95 and 96, seem to refer to some incident of a lascivious character, quite distinct from the liaison with the Dark Woman. After that the subject is absence and apologies for silence, which most students interpret as occasioned by a break in the friendship. Lastly we have the group (104-26) that brings section I to an end, and here all seems happiness once again. The affection between the friends is untroubled. The most interesting thing, however, about this last group is the number of sonnets it contains which seem to point to some season or year or occasion, either in the Friend's life or in public life generally. But before discussing all these matters, there is one major problem to be faced. When were the *Sonnets* begun? The answer to this is closely bound up with the problem of the identity of the Friend. It can, I think, be solved independently and it will be of great advantage to have it solved first, since if solved satisfactorily it narrows our field of choice in dealing with the identification.

In his edition of 1904, Beeching offers striking evidence on this matter, which has been strangely overlooked, largely I suspect because it has been regarded as one aspect of another kind of evidence (though he expressly warned against this). He calls his evidence 'the argument from repeated expression' and declares:

This argument must not be confused with an argument from what are called 'parallel passages'. It is primarily an argument from the use of identical words, only secondarily from similar ideas. . . . Of course it must be used with discretion. The repeated phrase of which notice is taken must be striking and individual. It would not do for example to suggest that sonnet 29 is of the same date as *Cymbeline* because in both the poet speaks of the lark as singing 'at heaven's gate'.

Perhaps the best way of bringing out the significance and true character of Beeching's method of dating is to compare his results with those of a critic who uses the ordinary method of parallel passages. That method, a complex of verbal parallels, parallelisms of thought and ideas, and metrical tests of various kinds, is elaborately discussed by Edmund Chambers, and forms to a large extent the basis of his well-known chronological table of the plays which is now widely accepted by scholars.[28] I myself find it more reliable for the plays after 1597 than before; it is demonstrably wrong, for example, in the placing of *Love's Labour's Lost* (which was certainly revised in part after the appearance of Gerard's *Herbal* in 1597).[29] And a chronology based upon tests applicable to dramas mainly in blank verse is manifestly unreliable for the dating of sonnets. Chambers admits this to a certain extent, for he writes 'Of the plays it is naturally only those with a strong love interest which are relevant'.[30] But since love is the element in which practically every sonnet of section I moves, it would be strange indeed if the parallel passages were not very numerous, or if Chambers did not discover about 150 parallels in plays like *The Two Gentlemen, Love's Labour's Lost, Romeo and Juliet,* and *A Midsummer Night's Dream.* What is needed for dating purposes in the *Sonnets* is plays with little or no love interest. The truth is that the ordinary parallel-passage tests in plays are largely irrelevant to the *Sonnets.* We must look for a new kind of touchstone altogether. And this Beeching discovered in repeated expression, which he thus expounds:

. . . Every writer knows the perverse facility with which a phrase once used presents itself again; and Shakespeare seems to have been not a little liable to this literary habit. It is not uncommon for him to use

[28] Chambers, *William Shakespeare,* I, 254 ff.
[29] See note on *Love's Labour's Lost* v. 2.590 (Cambridge New Shakespeare, 2nd edition), (1962).
[30] *William Shakespeare,* I, 254.

a word or phrase twice in a single play, and never afterwards. There is a strong probability, therefore, if a remarkable phrase or figure of speech occurs both in a sonnet and in a play, that the play and the sonnet belong to the same period. Now the greater number of the parallel passages hitherto recognised are to be found in *Henry IV,* in *Love's Labour's Lost,* and in *Hamlet;* and it is certain that *Henry IV* was written in 1597, that *Love's Labour's Lost* was revised in that same year, and that *Hamlet* is later still. To take an example: the phrase 'world-without-end' makes a sufficiently remarkable epithet; but it is so used only in Sonnet 57 and in *Love's Labour's Lost* (v. ii. 799). But as it is open to any one to reply that this and other phrases may have occurred in the original draft of the play, written several years earlier, it will be best to confine the parallels to *Henry IV,* the date of which is beyond dispute.

Compare, then, Sonnet 33—

> Anon *permit* the *basest* clouds to ride
> With ugly rack on his celestial face—

with *1 Henry IV,* i. ii. 221—

> the sun,
> Who doth *permit* the *base* contagious clouds,
> To smother up his beauty from the world.

Again, compare Sonnet 52—

> Therefore are *feasts* so *solemn* and so *rare,*
> Since, *seldom* coming, in the long year set
> . . . .
> So is the time that keeps you as my chest,
> Or as the wardrobe which the *robe* doth hide,
> To make some special instant special blest—

with *1 Henry IV,* iii. ii. 56—

My presence, like a *robe* pontifical,
Ne'er seen but wonder'd at; and so my state,
Seldom but sumptuous, showed like a *feast,*
And won by *rareness* such *solemnity*—

where the concurrence of the images of a feast and a
robe is very noticeable. Compare also Sonnet 64 with
2 Henry IV, III. i. 45, where the revolution of states is
compared with the sea gaining on the land, and the
land on the sea,—an idea not found in the famous description of the works of Time in *Lucrece* (937-59).[31]
Compare also the epithet 'sullen', applied to a bell in
Sonnet 71 and *2 Henry IV,* I. i. 102, and in the same
sonnet the phrase 'compounded with clay' or 'dust',
found in *2 Henry IV,* IV. v. 116, and *Hamlet,* IV. ii. 6.
The contrast between the canker or wild rose and the
cultivated rose, used so admirably in Sonnet 54, is
found again in *1 Henry IV,* I. iii. 176, and also in
Much Ado About Nothing I. iii. 28, a play written
probably a year or two years later. The very remarkable use of the word 'blazon', a technical term in her-
aldry, of the limbs of the human body, is found twice,
once in Sonnet 106, and once in *Twelfth Night,* I. v.
312, the date of which is probably 1600. Again, the
idea expressed in the phrases 'sick of welfare' or 'rank
of goodness' in Sonnet 118 is paralleled in *2 Henry IV,*
IV. ii. 64, 'sick of happiness', and in *Hamlet,* IV. vii.
118, 'goodness growing to a plurisy', and in these plays
only. The comparison of the eye in its socket to a star
moving in its 'sphere' is found only in Sonnets 119 and
in *Hamlet,* I. v. 17. In Sonnet 125 and in *Othello,* I.
i. 63, there is a conjunction of the word 'outward' with
the curious synonym 'extern' which occurs only in these
two places. I do not wish to press this argument further than it will go, but it must be allowed that its
force accumulates with every instance adduced; and,

[31] See below, page 104.

in my opinion, it is strong enough to dispose of the hypothesis that the main body of the sonnets was written in 1593 or 1594, especially as not a single argument has been brought forward for assigning them to so early a date, and every indication of both internal and external evidence suggests that they were written later.[32]

Lastly I may call Tyler as a witness on this matter of date. In 1599 Jaggard (as we have noted on p. 9) first printed sonnet 144, 'Two loves I have', from which we may gather that the Friend's intrigue with the Dark Woman was an established affair. Yet it had hardly been of long duration since lines 5-8 describe the 'worser spirit' actually then at work tempting his better angel,

> Wooing his purity with her foul pride.

The sonnet need not therefore have been written long before 1599. And the intrigue to which it alludes must have begun soon after the Poet and the Friend met, since the former complains in Sonnet 33 that when it came like a dark cloud into his life that Friend had been 'but one hour' his, which allowing for the exigencies of poetic metaphor might mean two or three months but scarcely more. Taking then the evidence of 144 and 33-6 together, it seems fair to assume that the two first met in 1599 or 1597, certainly not as far back as 1593-4.

Date-clues in group 97-126

So much for the beginning of the *Sonnets*. Can we find a like approximate date for the end? When for example was Shakespeare setting down that Envoy presumably intended to round off the frame-

[32] Beeching, *op. cit.*, Introduction, pp. xxiv-xxvii.

work sonnets, as Sidney had rounded off his *Astrophel and Stella*? An examination of the final sonnets 97-126 should provide the answer. For this group indisputably contains several date-clues, although the dates suggested have not been so far beyond dispute.

First of all in sonnet 98 we have an implied dating in the lines:

> From you I have been absent in the spring,
> When proud-pied April, dress'd in all his trim,
> Hath put a spirit of youth in every thing,
> That heavy Saturn laugh'd and leap'd with him

—lines in which Wyndham, interpreting them astrologically, found a reference to a certain day in one of the Aprils during the first three years of the seventeenth century. The date referred to may be 4 April 1600, 17 April 1601, or 29 April 1602; these being the only occasions during the period 1592 to 1609 when Saturn was seen to be 'in opposition' in the night sky. And as Wyndham justly observes, 'To have dragged in Saturn without reason or rhyme into a description of a particular month of April would have been a freak without precedent in Shakespeare,'[33] the more so that he did not use such terms lightly. 'Methinks I have astronomy' he remarks in sonnet 14, that is to say he was a student of astrology. And this being so, the most probable date would be 4 April 1600, the earliest upon which he observed the, saturnine planet leaping into the April sky, for by 17 April the phenomenon had become pedestrian.

[33] Wyndham, *op. cit.* pp. 244 ff. He cites Mr Heath of the Royal Observatory, Edinburgh, as his authority for these dates.

Yet sonnet 98 was not actually written on this date. All three, 97-99, are retrospective. Sonnet 97 tells us of an absence in some previous summer, 98 and 99 of absence in a previous spring. Furthermore, sonnet 99 is abnormal, having one line too many; and Beeching thinks it may represent an unfinished draft. But whatever be the explanation, the fact remains that Shakespeare was happily writing sonnets to the Friend about 1600.

The frequent apologies we saw above seem to show that the group covers a fairly long period during which Shakespeare wrote sonnets intermittently when he had time.[34] Tyler's claim that the group constitutes a single continuous poem can at any rate be ruled out, since it contains two sonnets (107, 124) which unquestionably allude to contemporary events (of different dates, I think), while 104 was clearly written to celebrate some definite occasion. Tyler accounts for this by claiming a single event, the Essex rising in 1601, as suitable for all three sonnets.[35] Chambers also associates 124 with Essex, not, however, with the rising but with his disgrace after returning from Ireland in 1598. But Chambers, like Tyler, is trying to find dates to suit his own conjectural dating of the *Sonnets* as a whole; whereas Beeching, who is influenced by no such theories, furnishes far the most plausible interpretation of 124, seeing it as an elaborate reference to the Gunpowder Plot of 1605. Here is the sonnet with Beeching's comments:

[34] See Tucker's important note on the servant-lord relation which the *Sonnets* imply (*op. cit.*).

[35] *Shakespeare's Sonnets,* edited by Thomas Tyler (1890).

If my dear love were but the child of state,
It might for Fortune's bastard be unfather'd,
As subject to Time's love or to Time's hate,
Weeds among weeds, or flowers with flowers gather'd.
No, it was builded far from accident;
It suffers not in smiling pomp, nor falls
Under the blow of thralled discontent,
Whereto th' inviting time our fashion calls.
It fears not Policy, that heretic,
Which works on leases of short numb'red hours,
But all alone stands hugely politic,
That it nor grows with heat, nor drowns with show'rs.
   To this I witness call the fools of time,
    Which die for goodness, who have liv'd for crime.

Pointing out that 'Love is the only true policy' is the obvious moral of the sonnet, Beeching holds that the state policy alluded to is the policy of 'the Jesuit conspirators whose object in life was to murder the king, and who when caught, posed as martyrs to the Faith. Such inconsistency of principle would justify the poet in calling them "the fools of time"[36] and pointing his moral with them.[37] And he interprets 'the blow of thralled discontent' as the Powder Plot in which the discontented 'party held down by penal enactments' planned to blow up Parliament including King, Lords and Commons. He hesitates to see in 'builded far from accident' an indirect allusion to the threatened Houses of Parliament, which were not so builded, but line 6 'in smiling pomp' seems to suit the ceremonial opening of Parliament, for which occasion the Plot was designed.

[36] I.e. persons deceived by the world in which they live.
[37] Beeching, *op. cit.*, note on lines 13-14.

If we accept this reading, as I think we may, important results follow. First, it implies that Shakespeare went on writing sonnets after James's accession, and at least seven years after he had written those 'sugred sonnets' known to Meres in 1598; second, all serious objections to the interpretation of sonnet 107 as a reference to the death of Elizabeth fall to the ground[38]; and third, it leaves us free to find a suitable date for sonnet 104, a date of capital importance as regards the dating of the *Sonnets* as a whole, inasmuch as the Poet states that this sonnet was written three years after he and the Friend first met. If the Farewell Sonnets were written in 1597-8 and the 'mortal moon' sonnet in 1603, sonnet 104 must lie somewhere between. As we may be able to fix a more exact date in the light of a conjectural identification of the Friend, we must next direct our attention to that problem.

[38] This sonnet will be considered in detail on page 89. Here it need only be observed that anyone who supposes the 'mortal moon' refers to the Spanish Armada which in 1588 sailed up the Channel in crescent formation has less astronomy than Shakespeare who, like all Elizabethans well seen in astrology, was especially interested in eclipses and knew very well that the moon is only eclipsed when full.

4

THE IDENTITY OF MR W. H.

Southampton pro and con

The time is now come to hang up a votive offering
in the cave of mystery or, to vary the metaphor, to
attempt to let in the light of history upon that
shadow in the cave that throws all the other shadows
into the shade; in a word, to answer the question,
who was this

Lascivious grace in whom all ill well shows—

this youth to whom Shakespeare paid tribute with
the finest love-poetry in the world, and such absolute homage that, as Valentine with Proteus, he was
ready to give him the woman he dearly loved? Unless all this was mere sycophancy to catch a patron,
a notion we have utterly rejected, the youth must
have been an unusual person, not only beyond all
measure handsome, but with intelligence and pow-

ers of appreciation—if far inferior to those of the mighty poet of the human heart' who lavished his adoration upon him—yet of sufficient quality to be invited to 'the marriage of true minds'. We have nothing to go upon but the *Sonnets* themselves, and the character of the Friend I have attempted to sketch from the hints they supply and they alone. And though, as any Shakespearian student must, I began with a vague idea as to a possible answer to the question, I had not proceeded far before coming to realise that an agnostic attitude was advisable.

Strange as it may seem, no one appears to have taken much interest in the question until Malone edited Thorpe's edition in 1780 and thus revealed for the first time the autobiographical character of the *Sonnets*. And even then it was hardly realised until Wordsworth in 1827 boldly declared

with this key
Shakespeare unlocked his heart; [1]

and by so doing unlocked the flood-gate through which an ever-broadening tide of speculation flowed until by 1944 it took thirty closely-packed pages in the second volume of an American edition of the *Sonnets* to record even brief extracts of the various theories about the identity of the Friend.

There they lie, the whole wilderness of them, for the inspection of curious eyes, a strange chapter in the history of human folly. In this study, however, apart from a passing reference to another 'Mr W. H.' whose claims to be 'the onlie begetter' were first put forth only the other day, I shall confine myself

[1] *Miscellaneous Sonnets,* Part II, 'Scorn not the sonnet'.

to the two who have divided the allegiance of most modern scholars: Henry Wriothesley (1573-1624), third Earl of Southampton, and William Herbert, who succeeded his father in 1601 as third Earl of Pembroke.

Southampton's claims were first advanced by Nathan Drake in 1817.[2] He seemed an obvious candidate. The Friend was clearly a man of high rank. Shakespeare had acknowledged Southampton as his patron by dedicating to him *Venus and Adonis* in 1593 and *The Rape of Lucrece* in 1594. Moreover, there is a striking parallel between the language of sonnet 26 and that of the prose dedication to *Lucrece*, which can scarcely be accidental, while, as many have observed, the general argument of sonnets 1-17, namely that 'nothing 'gainst Time's scythe can make defence Save breed', is anticipated or echoed in *Venus and Adonis*, lines 163-74:

Torches are made to light, jewels to wear,
Dainties to taste, fresh beauty for the use,
Herbs for their smell, and sappy plants to bear:
Things growing to themselves are growth's abuse.
  Seeds spring from seeds, and beauty breedeth beauty;
  Thou wast begot; to get it is thy duty.
Upon the earth's increase why shouldst thou feed,
Unless the earth with thy increase be fed?
By law of nature thou art bound to breed,
That thine may live when thou thyself art dead;
  And so in spite of death thou dost survive,
  In that thy likeness still is left alive.

and it is difficult to resist the impression of E. K. Chambers that the *Sonnets* were a 'continuation of

2 Nathan Drake, *Shakespeare and his Times* (1817).

74

the lyrical impulse represented by *Venus and Adonis*'.[3] Yet it is equally difficult not to agree with Beeching's assertion that 'their writing is distinctly finer than anything in the *Venus,* and the thought and experience are riper. The mastery of rhythm deepened in sonnet 5 and the melancholy of that and sonnet 12 point to a later date.'[4] Speaking generally, one has only to compare any of the first half dozen sonnets with the lines from *Venus* just quoted, and how much more elaborate, how highly wrought is their treatment. It looks as if the Poet had here taken up again and greatly developed subject-matter dealt with earlier, perhaps years earlier. The same explanation would also serve for the parallel between sonnet 26 and the dedication to *Lucrece*; what he had said well in prose came in useful again in a similar situation. This being so, the *Sonnets* might have been written for another nobleman altogether.

Other points have been often advanced against Southampton. The sonnets punning on the name Will[5] make it virtually certain that the youth's name was William. As for Thorpe's dedication 'to Mr W. H.',[6] whatever that may mean, it cannot possibly denote Master Henry Wriothesley. There is no evidence, again, that Southampton had any dealings with Shakespeare after 1594, the absence of any reference to him in the dedicatory material of the First Folio being particularly noticeable. On the

[3] Chambers, *William Shakespeare,* I, 564.

[4] Beeching, *op. cit.,* p. xxiv, n. 2.

[5] 135, 136 and 143. See Beeching, p. xxxii.

[6] Southamptonites try to escape from this dilemma by conjecturing that Thorpe obtained the *Sonnets* from Sir William Hervey, widower of the Countess of Southampton.

other hand the *Sonnets* contain no conceivable allusions to his courtship of Elizabeth Vernon, to his adoration of Essex, his attempt to take part in the Islands Voyage expedition, to the war in Ireland, or his part in the Essex putsch of 1601 and subsequent imprisonment. Above all, if we accept 1597-8 as the year in which Shakespeare began the *Sonnets*, he was at that date too old, being then twenty-four or twenty-five, while he must have been thirty or more when Shakespeare was writing his *Envoy* to his 'lovely boy'.

If Southampton, then, be ruled out we are left with William Herbert who succeeded his father as Earl of Pembroke in January 1601. Beeching, though no advocate of Southampton, and highly critical of Sidney Lee, could not find enough evidence to convince him that Herbert was the Friend. Nevertheless, there is more evidence in the *Sonnets* than he was aware of. Before coming to that, however, it will be helpful I think to look at the vivid picture we have of Herbert in later life.

Clarendon's portrait of Pembroke in his 'History of the Rebellion'

The Earl of Clarendon prefaces his famous history with an account of the chief persons at the English court immediately before the outbreak of the civil war, among whom William Herbert Earl of Pembroke stood pre-eminent. And if Shakespeare's young Friend did indeed grow up to become this great man, surely all we can learn about him is of first importance to students of the *Sonnets*. Yet the passage in Clarendon has been strangely neglected. Tyler and Leishman both give extracts but neither

76

Beeching nor Chambers mentions it and even Rollins dismisses it with the briefest reference. It is lengthy but should be made readily accessible. I am therefore printing it as a whole in an appendix, together with John Aubrey's 'brief life' of Pembroke, which supports Clarendon at all salient points.

If the child is father of the man, surely the man whom Clarendon gives us was offspring of the youth whose character we have attempted to build up or guess at from material supplied by the *Sonnets*. If ever, for instance, there was an 'Eve's apple', a lascivious grace, to tempt the young Eves at court with its beauty, it was Pembroke's. 'Immoderately given up to women', Clarendon tells us, yet never marrying except once, and then for property, since the wife was the daughter of the Earl of Shrewsbury and probably the richest heiress available—a marriage 'in which he was most unhappy'. It is noteworthy, too, that Clarendon, who knew all the court gossip, links this unhappiness with the sexual indulgence by explaining the latter as due either to 'his natural disposition or for want of his domestic content and delight'. Here the *Sonnets*, had he known them, might have taught him to leave the wife out, for the 'disposition' had been Herbert's from the age of adolescence, and sonnet 40 may well have supplied the key to it in the line

By wilful taste of what thyself refusest,

though the paradox involved must be left to psychologists to expound.

But there is the other side of the picture, and if the bad side helps us to identify the young Friend, may not the side that both Clarendon and Aubrey cannot praise enough help us to see, if only in germ, aspects of the boy's character we should not otherwise know, and to believe that his fascination for Shakespeare was by no means confined to a poet's worship of physical beauty? What a boy it must have been who became a few years later 'the most universally loved and esteemed of that age', the man who could live in the corrupt court of James I and not only escape corruption but help to purify the court by his presence in it, a man of such magnanimity and integrity that all could trust him never to seek his own interests or self-advancement, never to act out of private resentment or to curry favour with the king or his favourites; a man who, himself not without learning, could appreciate it in others, 'his conversation' being 'most with men of the most pregnant parts and understanding', while he was 'very liberal' towards such persons who had been recommended for his patronage; being indeed 'the greatest Maecenas to learned men of any peer of his time, or since. Finally, a man who was handsome and of a noble presence, and delighted in poetry and did sometimes write sonnets and epigrammes.'

After pondering these passages from Clarendon and Aubrey, many I think will be disposed to accept them as historical accounts of the person Shakespeare glorified in 126 sonnets.

Sonnets 1-17 and the youth's reluctance to marry

Let us now see, therefore, how far it is possible to trace allusions in the *Sonnets* to the events of his career as a young man. The main facts are to be found in state documents, in the shape of letters to correspondents in the country and abroad, including those from Rowland Whyte the agent of Herbert's uncle, Sir Robert Sidney, then at Flushing, and a few from Herbert himself to Cecil, and a very revealing one from Cecil to his friend Sir George Carew; and it is from these sources, or the bulk of them, that the story of the career has been told by two scholars, both Herbertists: namely Thomas Tyler in the edition of *Shakespeare's Sonnets*, 1890, and Edmund Chambers in his *William Shakespeare: A Study of Facts and Problems* (1930), together with its appendix *Shakespearean Gleanings* (1943). The account that follows attempts to combine both versions, which is not difficult, since one virtually begins where the other ends, according to the date they assign to the first meeting of Poet and Friend. For whereas Tyler, as we have seen, rightly assigns it to 1597–8, Chambers argues for 1595, and that for two reasons. One, because the records show Herbert, then fifteen, paying a visit in that year to court with his parents, to arrange for a marriage with Elizabeth, daughter of Sir George Carey, granddaughter of the Lord Chamberlain, who was the patron of Shakespeare's Company; and two, as seen above, because Chambers regarded the *Sonnets* as a product of the same poetic afflatus as gave us *Venus and Adonis*—an argument Beeching has already encountered, as we have also seen.

Chambers had already suggested this date in 1930 in his *William Shakespeare*. But a few years later, the recovery of fresh letters about the negotiations for Carey's daughter showed that they were broken off not, as had earlier appeared, on account of failure to agree about the property involved, but because of young Herbert's not 'liking' the lady when it came to the point. Accordingly, Chambers felt justified in summing up as follows when he returned to the problem in 1943.[7] 'There can be no certainty, but clearly Herbert's "not liking" brings us much nearer to the situation indicated by sonnets 1–17, than any other clue that has yet been suggested.' Yet though this seems to point towards the identification of the Friend with this youth averse to marrying, it tells us nothing about the date of the *Sonnets* themselves. These, Chambers assumed, began in 1595 and had ended by 1599; and though by way of winding up the story he goes on to mention later negotiations for Herbert's marriages and the Mary Fitton affair, he adds 'But these things lie outside the ambit of the *Sonnets*'—at the very moment at which Tyler and Beeching had shown the *Sonnets* actually began. Yet the discovery of negotiations as early as 1595, and in particular the cause of their breakdown, supplies an essential complement to Tyler's account. For it shows us that the negotiations of 1597 for a marriage with Bridget Vere, Burghley's granddaughter, which is where Tyler starts, was only the latest of a series of such attempts, and leaves little doubt in my mind that they all had broken down owing to young Herbert's 'not liking' the brides in question. It seems to me clear too from my reading of the evidence now seen as a whole, that sonnets 1-17 were written as a last resort to work upon the boy's imagination when all else had failed, and probably at the sug-

7 'The youth of the Sonnets' in *Shakespearean Gleanings* (1943).

gestion of his mother[8] who, as sister of the Sir Philip Sidney who wrote *The Defence of Poesie*, might well put some trust in such methods of persuasion. In a letter dated April 1597 we are told, 'My Lord Harbart hath with much adoe brought his father to consent that he may liue in London, yet not before next Springe',[9] and April 1598 may therefore be the date of the first meeting celebrated in sonnet 104 as having taken place three years earlier. Beeching, however, who without definitely committing himself to the Herbert side agrees that sonnets 1-17, urging the youth to marry, might have been written at Lady Pembroke's suggestion, throws out the idea that she invited the now famous poet of *Venus and Adonis* to Wilton for the purpose and that, if so, the first meeting may have taken place there.[10] That Shakespeare came to be familiar with Wilton seems borne out by the letter, now unhappily lost, but reported by William Cory as existing in 1885, in which Lady Pembroke, Sidney's sister, wrote to her son in December 1603, telling him to bring King James I, then staying at Salisbury, to Wilton to see *As You Like It,* and adding 'we have the man Shakespeare with us'.[11] It is unlikely that Shakespeare had not been acquainted before this with Wilton which, Aubrey tells us, was in Lady Herbert's time 'like a college, there were so many learned and ingeniose persons',[12] and who more

[8] Both Tyler (pp. 48-9) and Beeching (p. xxxix).
[9] See Tyler, p. 44.
[10] Beeching, *op. cit.* p. xxxix.
[11] See Chambers, *William Shakespeare,* I, 329.
[12] Aubrey, *Brief Lives,* edited O. Lawson Dick, p. 138.

'ingenious' than the writer for the Lord Chamberlain's company of players and author of *Venus and Adonis*? The 'man' was not of course of noble rank, scarcely indeed a gentleman; but could no doubt carry himself very agreeably in mixed company. Yet it seems to fit the facts better if we suppose that Shakespeare began the marriage series before he met Herbert, that the meeting happened soon after the youth arrived in London, that the series was then continued for a little while but discontinued at the request of the 'dear churl', after which a new series began with sonnet 18, 'Shall I compare thee to a summer's day'.

Herbert's father, now in failing health, was certainly anxious to see his heir suitably married and, after yielding to his importunity about coming up to London, was the more eager to have it all settled.

In any case, the summer of 1597 was occupied, according to the records, in negotiations for the wedding with Bridget Vere, granddaughter of the great Lord Burghley. But however it was, all the parents' efforts came to nothing. For after the negotiations had been going excellently for several months and Pembroke, Herbert's invalid father, is reported on 8 October to be 'resolved to accept Burghley's offer',[13] a fortnight later 'the matter is of a sudden quite dashed and in the opinion of the wise by great fault of Pembroke'; and Burghley thinks he was not well dealt with by Pembroke who refused his offer.[14]

'There is, of course,' writes Chambers, 'no suggestion here of Herbert's reluctance.' Yet is it not more

13 *Ibid.*
14 Chambers, *Shakespearean Gleanings,* p. 127.

82

than probable that the negotiations broke down for the same reason as before? To have told the great Lord Burghley that his granddaughter was 'not liked' would have been an insult. It was necessary for Pembroke to conclude the negotiations by suddenly raising his price. Burghley was angry, of course, but he would have been affronted had his Bridget been informed that the young man did not like her. In 1595 Pembroke had to break off the negotiations the same way in order not to cast any slur upon Elizabeth Carey, and it seems clear from the records that the girl's father attributed the breakdown entirely to a disagreement over the financial terms.

Finally it is worth noting that when in 1600 Sir Robert Sidney set negotiations on foot to marry his nephew, Herbert, to the niece of the Lord Admiral, his agent Robert Whyte was obliged to tell his master that he did not 'find any disposition in this gallant young lord to marry'.[15]

This disinclination to marry accounted not only for sonnets 1–17, but was the cause of their termination. But there was no disinclination on the part of this gallant and lascivious young lord to take anything that any woman would give him, and in the case of Mary Fitton it led him to disaster.

The Mary Fitton affair

Whether Shakespeare met him at Wilton or not, he was certainly doing so in London in the spring of 1598 when Herbert, leaving his sick father with his mother at Wilton, took up his residence in Baynards Castle.

[15] Chambers, *Shakespearean Gleanings,* p. 127.

What he did in 1598 there is little in the record to show. But we may place here the two episodes of the Rival Poet and the Dark Woman which the *Sonnets* reflect and relate, we have conjectured, especially to the Farewell series. Beeching's heading to the Farewell Sonnets runs *The Poet appeals against the Friend's Estrangement*—an estrangement, we may feel confident, not only or even perhaps mainly due to the influence of the Rival Poet, but to that of the Dark Woman. A young lord setting up house in London and wishing to cut a dash at court would have many preoccupations of greater immediate importance than keeping the friendship of his old player-poet in repair. Shakespeare gives us an idea of such preoccupations in the semi-satirical lines of sonnet 91:

Some glory in their birth, some in their skill,
Some in their wealth, some in their body's force;
Some in their garments, though new-fangled ill;
Some in their hawks and hounds, some in their horse.

And Rowland Whyte, Sir Robert Sidney's agent, gives us a further glimpse in his letter next year (1599), which speaks of the project of Herbert putting himself at the head of a bodyguard of two hundred horse to attend upon the queen, and of his 'swaggering it among the men of war'.[16] We read, too, in the letters of 1600 that, his parents remaining at Wilton, he was left free to do what he wished, and the fact that he accompanied Sir Charles Danvers (who was later executed for his part in the rising of Essex) on a visit to Lady Rich and Lady

16 See Tyler, *op. cit.*, p. 54.

Southampton at Gravesend, suggests that he was being tempted to associate with dangerous company. In fine, he yielded to a temptation of another but more characteristic sort, which was followed by a situation even more dangerous. For after making herself conspicuous as the leading lady in a masked dance before the queen at the wedding festivities on 16 June 1600 of a cousin of Herbert's, the lovely but wanton Mary Fitton found her way late at night and disguised as a man to Herbert's private quarters,[17] with the result that on 5 February next year, a fortnight after Herbert had succeeded his father as Earl of Pembroke, we find no less a person than Sir Robert Cecil casually remarking in a letter to a friend,

We have no news but that there is a misfortune befallen Mistress Fitton, for she is proved with child, and the Earl of Penbrooke being examined, confesseth a fact, but utterly renounceth all marriage. I fear they will both dwell in the Tower awhile, for the Queen hath vowed to send them thither.[18]

A later letter, written on 28 March, tells us that Pembroke was 'committed to the Fleet and that his cause [i.e. the woman responsible] is delivered of a boy who is since dead'. It may be that Mary Fitton, who belonged to one of the inferior ranks of the nobility hoped to better her condition by thus entangling a young and wealthy nobleman. If so, the gamble failed utterly; she had no putative heir to offer him and he had already refused to be caught

17 *Ibid.*, p. 57.
18 See Tyler, p. 56.

85

by the claims of honour and decency which her family urged upon him. For as ever he refused any marrying. Yet he, too, paid; and after serving a term in prison he was banished to the country and there he languished so long as the queen lived.

Now this collapse in the young Earl's fortunes just at the outset of what promised to be the loftiest of careers, together with his enforced absence from London, seems to afford a ready explanation of the supposed 'break' in the Absence Sonnets (97 etc.). In other words, I am persuaded by my friend Blair Leishman[19] that sonnets 94, 95, 96 are discreet, if deliberately obscure, reflections of the Fitton affair, though in the wrong order, and that 95 and 96 were written in 1600 or early 1601 when the rumours of her midnight visit to Herbert, which are known to have been current among the gossip-mongers shortly after, were reaching Shakespeare's ears; but that 94 belongs to the end of March 1601 when the full horror of the situation was clear to the whole world. That the little group of 'licentious grace' sonnets had nothing to do with the liaison group is proved by their tone of affectionate indulgence. Shakespeare, in fact, writes like a worldly-wise uncle giving advice to a favourite nephew, almost like Lord Chesterfield writing to his son. Sonnet 93, with its reference to a deceived husband, shows he had not forgotten the youth's theft of his mistress, but we learnt in 34 and 35 that he had forgiven, and the boy had repented with tears. Yet reproof there is, unhesitating and unconcealed. In 94, which is a development of the charge of 'wilful taste of what

[19] In personal talk shortly before the accident that led to his death.

86

thyself refusest' in sonnet 40. 8, the young earl is told by inference that he is given to the detestable practice of enjoying women out of mere curiosity, which is very much what Clarendon tells us about Pembroke.

Occasions in the Final Group

If all the foregoing be granted and Pembroke be accepted as the Friend, the rest of the sonnets that seem to point to definite dates or occasions fall into place. To begin with, sonnet 104, a birthday sonnet I think, speaking of having first met the Friend in April three years earlier, must have been written in April 1601 and points to April 1598 as the time of the first meeting. But in April 1601 the young earl had just fallen out of favour at court owing to the Fitton scandal, and at such a time this affectionate greeting from his poet-player must have been peculiarly acceptable. Others of Pembroke's friends took the opportunity of assuring him of their continued admiration. For example, Francis Davison, son of Secretary Davison, thus addressed Pembroke in dedicating *The Poetical Rhapsody* to him in 1602:

> Great earl, whose high and noble mind is higher,
> And nobler than thy noble high desire;
> Whose outward shape, though it most lovely be,
> Doth in fair robes a fairer soul attire. . . .[20]

After all, Pembroke was by no means the first of Elizabeth's courtiers to get one of her maids into trouble; his position as earl was unassailable and the disgrace could only be temporary.

[20] Quoted from Beeching, *op. cit.* p. xxxviii.

If sonnet 124 makes use, as we have seen, of allusions to the Gunpowder Plot of 5 November 1605, it would seem that Shakespeare ceased writing sonnets to Pembroke about 1606. Indeed sonnet 125 seems to hint that his praise of the Friend's beauty by this date were growing stale in men's eyes and prompted in part by self-interest—'mixed with seconds'. Thus sonnets 100 to 106 would cover the period of 1601 to 1606. They were therefore written intermittently and confessedly so, in contrast with the Poet's earlier activity, when

> Our love was new, and then but in the spring,
> When I was wont to greet it with my lays.[21]

No doubt both men were extremely busy. During these years Shakespeare was writing and producing his greatest tragedies and Pembroke had more than enough to do if he was to steer a path of integrity and honour for himself through the muddy waters of James's court. And so we get sonnets apologising for long silence, for the poverty of his invention, for allowing other claims, the claims of his profession as actor-dramatist, love affairs—all after the conventionally traditional fashion of the poet in 'service' to his lord, as explained by Tucker above.

Among them, however, are other sonnets that glow with a peculiarly emotional or joyous quality. Such is the birthday greeting just noticed. Another is the splendid sonnet 116,

> Let me not to the marriage of true minds
> Admit impediments

21 This refers, I think, to the aubade or dawn-song.

—one of the finest and most 'universal' love sonnets in the whole collection. It must, nevertheless, I feel, have been composed for a special occasion, as when the young earl had conferred upon his poet some conspicuous token of his appreciation, one of those 'favours' that Heminge and Condell speak of in the dedication to the First Folio; perhaps an enthusiastic letter in praise of the performance of a play, for by this time he would have been growing increasingly proud of his beloved poet-player's triumphs. But when rightly understood the much debated sonnet 107 is an example of pure joy, jubilation indeed, which they both shared. One of the results of having settled the dating of the *Sonnets* as a whole and the identity of the Poet's Friend is that it enables us to accept as certain the occasion of sonnet 107, which, though bandied about in recent years by critics in order to accord it with their own dating, has always been obvious to readers of common sense. I mean the death of the aged Queen Elizabeth on 24 March 1603.

Think what that meant for Pembroke! He could return to London from his banishment, and at once take his rightful place at court with a king on the throne favourable to himself and his friends. As for Shakespeare, the last days of Elizabeth make an obscure chapter of his life. He seems not to have been held guilty for the performance of *Richard II*, with its deposition scene, on the eve of the abortive rising of Essex; but she obviously could have harboured no kindly feelings towards the author, if she knew who he was. In any case James at once showed him much good will: the Company became His Majesty's Players, and the principal actors,

Shakespeare among them, were created Grooms of the Chamber. The whole country too seemed to share a similar good fortune, for as the queen lay dying no one but Robert Cecil knew who would succeed or what fate or even what form of religion awaited England. Thus, all was in doubt, speculation ran riot, a number of possible heirs 'gaped' for the throne; so that a great fear oppressed men's hearts, while the astrologers prognosticated that terrible disasters would follow the queen's death. A sigh, therefore, of immense relief greeted the arrival of the ungainly Scot, whose coronation settled the succession for good (or, as Shakespeare put it, incertainties crowned themselves assured) and whose first act was to declare that he had come to bring peace not only to England, to Britain, but to the whole of Europe—a peace that would last for ever. It was a balmy time indeed: the very season, an unusually mild spring, seemed to share in the joy and those who had prophesied evil now laughed at their own forecasts.

Such was the general sense of the sonnet in relation to the affairs of state. Meanwhile this chapter may be appropriately rounded off with the concluding couplet of the sonnet—which combines both its public and its personal significance:

> And thou in this shalt find thy monument
> When tyrants' crests and tombs of brass are spent.

The lines are a variation of the famous Horatian claim in the Odes, III. 30, that in his verses he has created a monument more durable than brass, a claim which Shakespeare has transferred to the eternal beauty of his Friend in several earlier sonnets. But here the loan from Horace is given a double meaning since the 'monumentum aere' is that of the tyrant queen.

5

THEMES AND SOURCES

One of the tasks laid upon a competent editor of a Shakespeare play is to provide some account of its source (or sources) and a discussion of the nature and extent of the dramatist's debt to it; while 'source' in this sense should embrace not merely the books or pervious dramas from which he presumably drew his material, but also (even more important, if far less easy to determine with any precision), the mediaeval or sixteenth-century ideas and assumptions he entertained, without some knowledge of which the play in question cannot be fully understood.

Somewhat analogous problems face an editor of the *Sonnets,* both as regards their main and recurrent themes and in connection with points that may crop up in individual sonnets. Two questions of major relevance must be taken up at this point. The first is: What themes, etc., does Shakespeare as a sonneteer owe to earlier writers of sonnets, or other classical and Renaissance poems? There are some critics, indeed, Sidney Lee in particular, who hold that the *Sonnets* are merely imitative, a tissue of echoes and borrowings from the Italian and French sonneteers who had been celebrating their ladies or their patrons since the thirteenth century. This view has been already discussed above, and is now I believe no longer held by any reputable critic. On the other hand, poets of all periods who, like Shakespeare, propose to immortalise their beloved or even themselves in verse inevitably have recourse to similar imagery and ideas without any question of imitation or borrowing at all. This similarity of treatment is the subject of a stimulating and learned book by Mr J. B. Leishman entitled *Themes and Variations in Shakespeare's Sonnets* (1961). His principal concern is with the theme of poetry, and of course love-poetry as a defier of Time, which devours all things, or with the kindred theme of poetry that confers immortality upon the person addressed: a theme best expressed in sonnets 18 and 19, the first of Shakespeare's real love-sonnets. For he has suddenly dropped the advice to marry, which he had been commissioned to impart, and which he had given in seventeen sonnets; and has turned to the adoration of the beloved. He sums it up in the couplet of sonnet 19 which, after a dozen lines exemplifying the ruthless omnipotence of devouring Time, contemptuously exclaims

Yet, do thy worst, old Time. Despite thy wrong,
My love shall in my verse ever live young.

Leishman's purpose being not to edit but to illustrate, he is primarily interested in parallels and affinities in the sonnets of Shakespeare's predecessors: Horace and Ovid, Petrarch, Tasso and Ronsard, Sidney and Spenser, Daniel and Drayton, to name the chief only. But when, as he could hardly have avoided doing at times, he came face to face with the question of whether Shakespeare had actually read this or that of his forerunners, the answer varies in cogency. The evidence for example as regards the Italian poets, even Petrarch, is so uncertain as to be virtually negative. It seems pretty conclusive, on the other hand, for Ronsard—it being clear at any rate that sonnet 74 is to some extent connected with the *Elegie à Marie*. Yet in this case both Shakespeare and Ronsard appear to go back to Ovid, a point to which we must return.

As for the English predecessors, we cannot doubt that Shakespeare read them eagerly, without necessarily paying them the compliment of imitation. In one instance indeed he only borrowed to make fun of the writer in question. Thomas Watson was a pretentious poetaster who came early into the field with a sonnet sequence published in 1582 under the title of the ΕΚΑΤΟΜΠΑΘΙΑ or *Passionate Centurie of Love,* the seventh 'Passion' running as follows:

> Harke you that list to heare what sainte I serue:
> Her yellowe lockes exceede the beaten goulde;
> Her sparkeling eies in heau'n a place deserue;
> Her forehead high and faire of comely moulde;
>   Her wordes are musicke all of siluer sounde;
>   Her wit so sharpe as like can scarse be found:
> Each eybrowe hanges like *Iris* in the skies;

Her *Eagles* nose is straight of stately frame;
On either cheeke a *Rose* and *Lillie* lies;
Her breath is sweete perfume, or hollie flame;
   Her lips more red than any *Corall* stone;
    Her necke more white, then aged *Swans* yat mone;
Her brest transparent is, like *Christall* rocke;
Her fingers long, fit for *Apolloes* Lute;
Her slipper such as *Momus* dare not mocke;
Her vertues all so great as make me mute:
   What other partes she hath I neede not say,
   Whose face alone is cause of my decaye.

Turn now to Shakespeare's description of his Dark Woman in sonnet 130, beginning 'My mistress' eyes are nothing like the sun', and it will be seen that it parodies all but one of Watson's lines.[1] And there are other signs that Shakespeare had read and marked his Watson. For instance, when Rosalind says of a lover that 'Cupid hath clapped him o'th' shoulder' [2] she seems to be echoing a line from the first 'Passion'.

But Shakespeare was already eighteen when Watson's *Centurie* appeared on the book-stalls; and a volume entitled *Songes and Sonettes, written by the ryght honourable Lorde Henry Haward late Earle of Surrey, and other Apud Richardum Tottel,* commonly known today as *Tottel's Miscellany,* had taken London by storm in 1557, a few years before he was born, and went through eight editions before 1591, when Sidney's *Astrophel and Stella* appeared; which publication is usually taken as the beginning of the Elizabethan sonnet craze. Know-

---

1 Pointed out by Patrick Cruttwell, *The Shakespearean Moment* (1954), p. 18.
2 *As You Like It,* IV. i. 46.

ing as they now do that Wyatt and Surrey were writing sonnets in the third and fourth decades of the sixteenth century, scholars imagine a gap of a whole generation—more than a quarter of a century—between them and Sidney. Surely the immense vogue of *Tottel's Miscellany* has been strangely ignored. During these forty years it had become part of the popular literature of the country. Surrey's Geraldine had become a legendary figure, a kind of English Laura, before Nashe published his *Jack Wilton* in 1593.[3] If Shakespeare may be taken as a witness, lovers in the provinces about 1600 still took it with them when they went a-courting,[4] and the very gravediggers sang snatches of it as they 'built houses that last till doomsday'.[5] Addressing the 'gentle reader' in his preface, the worthy Tottel claims it

not euill doon, to publish, to the honor of the Englishe tong, and for profit of the studious of Englishe eloquence, those workes which the vngentle hoorders vp of such treasure haue heretofore enuied thee.[6]

Who these 'ungentle hoorders' may have been is unknown, but the expression leaves us asking whether any reader, even Sidney himself, would have had access to Surrey's poems if Tottel had not printed the text three years after he was born. And one can guess with what delight the lad at Stratford, his junior by ten years, might have come upon

3 See *Works of Nashe,* edited by R. B. McKerrow, IV, 252 ff.

4 *The Merry Wives of Windsor,* I. i. 184.

5 *Hamlet,* V. i. 61 ff.

6 Sidney Lee, 'The Elizabethan Sonnet', *Cambridge History of English Literature,* III, 247.

Surrey's 'Description and praise of his loue Geraldine':

> From Tuskane came my Ladies worthy race:
> Faire Florence was sometyme her auncient seate:
> The Western yle, whose pleasaunt shore dothe face
> Wilde Cambers clifs, did geue her liuely heate:
> Fostered she was with milke of Irishe brest:
> Her sire, an Erle: her dame, of princes blood.
> From tender yeres, in Britain she doth rest,
> With kinges childe, where she tasteth costly food.
> Honsdon did first present her to mine yien:
> Bright is her hewe, and Geraldine she hight.
> Hampton me taught to wishe her first for mine:
> And Windsor, alas, dothe chase me from her sight.
> Her beauty of kind her vertues from aboue.
> Happy is he, that can obtaine her loue.

or his 'Vow to loue faithfully howsoever he be rewarded', a page or two further on:

> Set me wheras the sunne doth parche the grene,
> Or where his beames do not dissolue the yse:
> In temperate heate where he is felt and sene:
> In presence prest of people madde or wise.
> Set me in hye, or yet in lowe degree:
> In longest night, or in the shortest daye:
> In clearest skye, or where clowdes thickest be:
> In hasty youth, or when my heeres are graye.
> Set me in heauen, in earth, or els in hell,
> In hyll, or dale, or in the fomying flood:
> Thrall, or at large, aliue where so I dwell:
> Sicke, or in health: in euyll fame, or good.
> Hers will I be, and onely with this thought
> Content my selfe, although my chaunce be nought.

Professor Prince calls this sonnet 'conventional' but, as he shows, Surrey had achieved the form of the

English sonnet by learning from the fumbling attempts by Wyatt.[7] And Shakespeare learned from Surrey and followed much the same rhetorical pattern as Surrey used in this last sonnet when he came to write his own sonnets 66 and 129.

But perhaps the most important effect of Tottel's publication is that it determined the form of the English sonnet, viz. three quatrains of ten-syllabled lines, concluding with a couplet, as opposed to the Italian form of two parts, an octave consisting of two quatrains and a sextet of two tercets. The latter was far more complicated than the one Wyatt and Surrey between them developed, and the proof that their form was the one suited to the genius of the English language[8] is shown by the fact that only one of their English successors adopted the Petrarchian sonnet. Apart from one or two sporadic examples, the only poet to write consistently in the Italian form is Henry Constable, whose sonnet-sequence *Diana* was published about 1594. More significantly perhaps, George Gascoigne, whose *Posies* (1575) contained 'certain Notes of Instruction concerning the Making of Verse', seems to ignore any but the English form, since he writes

Some thinke that all Poemes (being short) may be called Sonets, as in deede it is a diminutive word derived of *Sonare*, but yet I can beste allowe to call those Sonets whiche are of fourtene lynes, every line conteyning tenne syllables. The firste twelve do ryme in

[7] F. T. Prince, *The Sonnet from Wyatt to Shakespeare* in Stratford-upon-Avon Studies, 2 (1960).

[8] See Matthew Black, *Elizabethan and Seventeenth Century Lyrics* (1938), pp. 40, 51-2.

staves of foure lines by crosse meetre, and the last twoo ryming togither do conclude the whole.[9]

That Shakespeare read his Sidney, his Spenser, his Daniel and his Drayton, together with other English sonnet-writers, among his elders and contemporaries, goes without saying. But though it is clear that both Daniel and Drayton learned from him, what he may have owed to them seems quite uncertain[10]; and naturally none of them offered him material for scorn as Watson had done. It is not that there were no parallels or affinities, but that as in the case of Ronsard it is often possible to trace them to Ovid and/or Horace from whom Shakespeare may have derived them directly—which brings us to the capital problem of Shakespeare's sources in the *Sonnets*, what Leishman calls his 'main subject',[11] namely Shakespeare's relation in the *Sonnets* to Ovid and Horace, and in particular what his 'resonant claims' to be conferring immortality in defiance of Time that devours all things owes to the great Roman poets.

It has always been known that Ovid's *Metamorphoses* was one of the dramatist's principal source-books, in making use of which he relied chiefly but not entirely upon Golding's English translation.[12] And Leishman underlines the close connection between the great sonnets 64, 65 and Ovid's epilogue

[9] George Gascoigne, *Posies,* edited by J. W. Cunliffe (1907), pp. 471-2.

[10] Leishman, *Themes and Variations in Shakespeare's Sonnets,* p. 30.

[11] Leishman, *op. cit.,* p. 30.

[12] See my article on 'Shakespeare's "small Latin"—how much?' in *Shakespeare Survey,* x, pp. 12 ff.

to the final book of the *Metamorphoses*. He is, too,
I think, the first to detect an unmistakable echo of
Ovid in the tender 63. But though he quotes sonnet
64[13] he does not appear to notice that this, too,
derives direct from Ovid, is indeed virtually a translation of earlier lines of the same final book. Nor
has he observed that Sidney Lee had been before
him here and driven the point firmly home.

The truth is that one of Lee's best treatments of
the *Sonnets* has been generally overlooked because
it was not published until after his death, in a
volume of his essays edited by F. S. Boas.[14] The
strength of Lee's argument lies in the close verbal
parallelisms he notes between Shakespeare and
Golding, which leave no doubt that the main, if
not the only, source of the great sonnets on Time
the devourer was the English version of Ovid. Examples are:

Golding XV, 984-995: Ovid, xv, 871ff.

Now have I brought a woork too end which neither
    Ioues feerce wrath,
Nor sword, nor fyre, nor freating age with all the force
    it hath
Are able too abolish quyght. Let comme that fatall
    howre
Which (saving of this brittle flesh) hath over mee no
    powre,
And at his pleasure make an end of myne uncerteyne
    tyme.
Yit shall the better part of mee assured bee too clyme
Aloft above the starry skye. And all the world shall
    never

13 Leishman, *op. cit.* pp. 32-3.
14 *Elizabethan and other Essays* (1929).

100

Be able for to quench my name. For looke how farre
  so ever
The Roman Empyre by the ryght of conquest shall ex-
  tend,
So farre shall all folke read this woork. And tyme with-
  out all end
(If Poets as by prophesie about the truth may ame)
My lyfe shall everlastingly bee lengthened still by fame.

Sonnet 55

Not marble nor the gilded monuments
Of princes shall outlive this pow'rful rhyme;
But you shall shine more bright in these contents
Than unswept stone, besmear'd with sluttish time.
When wasteful war shall statues overturn,
And broils root out the work of masonry,
Nor Mars his sword nor war's quick fire shall burn
The living record of your memory.
'Gainst death and all-oblivious enmity
Shall you pace forth; your praise shall still find room,
Even in the eyes of all posterity
That wear this world out to the ending doom.
    So, till the judgment that yourself arise,
    You live in this, and dwell in lovers' eyes.

While Leishman refers once again to Ovid's
'impressive discourse on mutability which meant
so much to Spenser and other Elizabethans', and
notes that this passage from book xv of the *Metamorphoses* (like the conclusion about Poetry as the
defier of Time) must have been much in Shakespeare's memory, he has not observed how closely
that memory clung to the actual words of Golding.
Lee spends the rest of his remarkable essay in elabo-
rating this matter. I content myself here with one
or two instances of Shakespeare's use of Ovid's vivid

101

physiographic proofs of his central cosmic theory. The ceaseless recurrence of natural phenomena is illustrated by Ovid from the example of the sea-waves' motion. Golding translates the passage

As every wave drives others forth, and that that comes
 behind
Both thrusteth and is thrust himself; even so the times
 by kind
Do fly and follow both at once and evermore renew.

Shakespeare presents the argument less methodically, but he adopts the illustrative figure without much disguise. Thus he begins sonnet 60:

Like as the waves make towards the pebbled shore,
So do our minutes hasten to their end;
Each changing place with that which goes before,
In sequent toil all forwards do contend.

Even more striking is Shakespeare's reproduction of Ovid's graphic description of the constant encroachment of land on sea and sea on land, which the Latin poet adduces as fresh evidence of matter's endless variations, and fortifies by a long series of professed personal observations. In Golding's rendering the passage opens thus:

Even so have places oftentimes exchanged their estate,
For I have seen it sea which was substantial ground
 alate.
Again, where sea was, I have seen the same become dry
 land.

In sonnet 64 Shakespeare assimilates these words with a literalness which makes him claim to 'have seen' with his own eyes the phenomena of Ovid's narration:

> When I have seen the hungry ocean gain
> Advantage on the kingdom of the shore,
> And the firm soil win of the wat'ry main,
> Increasing store with loss, and loss with store;
> When I have seen such interchange of state . . .

The driving vigour with which Ovid pursues this corroborative theme of 'interchange' or 'exchange' between earth and ocean is well reflected in the swing of Golding's ballad metre:

> And in the tops of mountains high old anchors have been found,
> Deep valleys have by watershot been made of level ground,
> And hills by force of gulling oft have into sea been worne,
> Hard gravel ground is sometime seen where marish was beforne.

With especial force does Ovid point to the subsidence of land beneath the voracious sea:

> Men say that Sicil also hath been joined to Italy
> Until the sea consumed the bounds between, and did supply
> The room with water. If ye go to seek for Helice
> And Bury, which were cities of Achaea, you shall see
> Them hidden under water; and the shipmen yet do show
> The walls and steeples of the towns drowned under as they row.[15]

15 Lee, *Elizabethans and other Essays*, pp. 129-30.

Lee discovers a reflection of what he calls 'Ovid's metaphysical or physical interpretation of the universe' in some fifteen of the *Sonnets*. He also finds the same influence in the passage of *2 Henry IV* (III. i. 45 ff.) already referred to on p. 66. Leishman has missed a good deal of this because of his preoccupation with Horace and more particularly with his ode 30 in book III, which begins

exegi monumentum aere perennius.

It is an ode, as is well known, which inspired the similar vaunt with which Ovid concluded his immortal *Metamorphoses,* and Leishman sees it as the inspiration likewise of sonnet 55, which he twice refers to as echoing the 'Horatian resonance': but as we have seen Shakespeare caught the resonance at second hand inasmuch as the sonnet is virtually a paraphrase of Ovid's lines.

Yet though the influence of Horace may have been mainly indirect, it was certainly direct also. 'Was Shakespeare familiar with Horace's Odes?' asks Leishman. 'I can see no way of proving that he was, but, on the other hand, it seems to me almost incredible that he should not have been.' [16] In his much neglected essay on *Shakespeare's Significances*[17] Edmund Blunden furnished the proof that Leishman sought, by demonstrating that in *Lear* III. iv the King is reminded of one of Horace's Epistles by the name of a fiend 'poor Tom' bor-

[16] *Op. cit.* p. 36.
[17] A lecture delivered before the Shakespeare Association in 1929, reprinted in *The Mind's Eye* (1934) and again in Bradby, *Shakespearian Criticism 1919-35.*

rowed from Harsnett and at III. vi. 78-80 himself refers to the last ode of book I 'Persicos odi, puer, apparatus', known to any schoolboy, when he bids Edgar change his garments.[18] Thus though it is impossible to trace the influence of Horace in the *Sonnets* we may rest assured that Shakespeare had once read a little Horace at school.

It should be added that Thomas Tyler, who anticipated so much modern criticism in the Introduction to his edition of the *Sonnets* published in 1890, has in a sense anticipated Lee by insisting upon Shakespeare's debt to Ovid and Horace. But sharing the accepted opinion of his age, he refused to believe this influence could have been direct and threw out the ingenious suggestion that Shakespeare derived the 'small Latin' he made use of in the *Sonnets,* and especially sonnet 55, from Meres (who in dealing with Shakespeare among other poets quotes both the Horatian *exegi monumentum* and the famous vaunt of Ovid at the conclusion of the *Metamorphoses*). But in face of the far greater quantity and variety of the parallels cited by Lee it is clear that if there were any borrowing it was Meres who borrowed from the *Sonnets* and not vice versa.

[18] See also *King Lear* (Cambridge New Shakespeare), notes on III. iv. 144, and III. vi. 78-80.

APPENDIX

Clarendon's Description of William Herbert

After describing the character of the detestable, insolent and unpopular Earl of Arundel, Clarendon continues:

William earl of Pembroke was next, a man of another mould and making, and of another fame and reputation with all men, being the most universally loved and esteemed of any man of that age; and, having a great office in the Court, [he] made the Court itself better esteemed and more reverenced in the country. And as he had a great number of friends of the best men, so no man had ever the wickedness to avow himself to be his enemy. He was a man very well bred, and of excellent parts, and a graceful speaker upon any subject, having a good proportion of learning, and a ready wit to apply it and enlarge upon it; of a pleasant and facetious humour, and a disposition affable, generous, and magnificent. He was master of a great fortune from his ancestors, and had a great addition by his wife (another daughter and heir of the earl of Shrewsbury), which he enjoyed during his life, she outliving him: but all served not his expense, which was only limited by his great mind and occasions to use it nobly.

He lived many years about the Court before in it, and never by it; being rather regarded and esteemed by King James than loved and favoured: and after the foul fall of the earl of Somerset, he was made Lord Chamberlain of the King's house more for the Court's sake than his own; and the Court appeared with the more lustre because he had the government of that province. As he spent and lived upon his own fortune, so he stood upon his own feet, without any other support than of his proper virtue and merit; and lived towards the favourites with that decency as would not suffer them to censure or reproach his master's judgment and election, but as with men of his own rank. He was exceedingly beloved in the Court, because he never desired to get that for himself which others laboured for, but was still ready to promote the pretences of worthy men. And he was equally celebrated in the country for having received no obligations from the Court which might corrupt or sway his affections and judgment; so that all who were displeased and unsatisfied in the Court or with the Court were always inclined to put themselves under his banner, if he would have admitted them; and yet he did not so reject them as to make them choose another shelter, but so far to depend on him that he could restrain them from breaking out beyond private resentments and murmurs.

He was a great lover of his country, and of the religion and justice which he believed could only support it; and his friendships were only with men of those principles. And as his conversation was most with men of the most pregnant parts and understanding, so towards any who needed support or encouragement, though unknown, if fairly recommended to him, he was very liberal. And sure never man was planted in a Court that was fitter for that soil, or brought better qualities with him to purify that air.

Yet his memory must not be so flattered that his virtues and good inclinations may be believed without some allay of vice, and without being clouded with great infirmities, which he had in too exorbitant a proportion. He indulged to himself the pleasures of all kinds, almost in all excesses. Whether out of his natural constitution, or for want of his domestic content and delight, (in which he was most unhappy, for he paid much too dear for his wife's fortune by taking her person into the bargain,) he was immoderately given up to women. But therein he likewise retained such a power and jurisdiction over his very appetite, that he was not so much transported with beauty and outward allurements, as with those advantages of the mind as manifested an extraordinary wit and spirit and knowledge, and administered great pleasure in the conversation. To these he sacrificed himself, his precious time, and much of his fortune. And some who were nearest his trust and friendship were not without apprehension that his natural vivacity and vigour of mind began to lessen and decline by those excessive indulgences.[1]

A few sentences from Aubrey's *Brief Lives*[2] may finally be quoted to supplement Clarendon's

[1] Clarendon, *History of the Rebellion,* ed. W. Dunn Macray (Oxford, 1888), I, 71-3.

[2] Aubrey, *op. cit.,* edited by O. Lawson Dick (1949), pp. 144-6.

account. Aubrey says that Pembroke and his brother
Philip

were the most popular Peers in the West of England;
but one might boldly say, in the whole Kingdome. . . .
Earle William entertained at Wilton, at his own Cost,
King James the first, during the space of many moneths.
King Charles 1st loved Wilton above all places and
came thither ever sommer. . . . William Herbert, Earl
of Pembroke was a most noble Person and the Glory of
the Court. . . . He was handsome, and of an admirable presence. He was the greatest Maecenas to
learned Men of any Peer of his time: or since. He was
very generous and open-handed: He gave a noble Collection of choice Bookes, and Manuscripts to the Bod-
laean Library at Oxford. . . . He was a good Scholar,
and delighted in Poetrie: and did sometimes (for his
Diversion) write some Sonnets and Epigrammes, which
deserve Commendation. . . . Wilton will appeare to
have been an Academie, as well as Palace, and was (as
it were) the Apiarie, to which Men, that were excellent
in Armes, and Arts, did resort, and were caress't; and
many of them received honourable Pensions.

Due